D0903396

INFANCY

GARLAND REFERENCE LIBRARY
OF SOCIAL SCIENCE
(VOL. 324)

INFANCY
A Guide to Research and Resources

Hannah Nuba-Scheffler, M.S.
Deborah Lovitky Sheiman, Ed.D.
Kathleen Pullan Watkins, Ed.D.

Garland Publishing, Inc. • New York & London
1986

Library of Congress Cataloging-in-Publication Data

Scheffler, Hannah Nuba, 1924–
    Infancy : a guide to research and resources.

    (Garland reference library of social science ;
vol. 324)
    Includes bibliographies and indexes.
    1. Infants—Development.   2. Infants—Development—
Bibliography.   I. Sheiman, Deborah Lovitky.
II. Watkins, Kathleen Pullan.   III. Title.   IV. Series:
Garland reference library of social science ; v. 324.
HQ774.S34   1986   305.2′32   86-9970
ISBN 0-8240-8699-6 (alk. paper)

Cover design by Renata Gomes

Printed on acid-free, 250-year-life paper
Manufactured in the United States of America

Contents

Preface

Infancy, the first stage of human life, lasts approximately two years postbirth. It has only been since the end of World War II that professionals have sought information on how an infant functions and what abilities and capacities an infant holds.

Medical progress to maintain life and detect high-risk pregnancies and births, a social climate that brought the emergence of women's liberation and with it infant-toddler child care, and educational interventions (in the form of books and toys) that stirred parents to enrich their infants' cognitive and social development all generated interest in the tiny being called *baby*. "Infant" comes from the Latin *infans, infantis*, meaning "without speech."

Though infancy is technically the period between birth and age two, this book has addressed development beginning at the prenatal period--the nine months from conception to birth. Crucial events that take place during this period can affect birth and growth.

Change from conception through infancy is more dramatic and extreme than at any other phase in the human life span. The infant goes from being prone to the ability to stand upright. The size and the shape of the body changes. The complexity of sensory and perceptual abilities increases. The tie or bond to other humans, particularly those who give consistent care, concern, and love appears. The need to know and master concepts, tasks, and objects develops. Language grows and speech emerges, and through all this arises an individual--a social human being with unique personal characteristics and styles.

These rapid developmental changes during infancy account for the many questions parents ask, the fascination of researchers to explore, scrutinize, and examine infant behavior, and the authors' need to provide parents and others concerned with the infant a broadly conceived book.

Infancy: A Guide to Research and Resources has two main goals. One is to present a brief, simplified view of current data on the functioning of infants. The second is to allow the reader to examine the topics or subtopics of interest by selecting appropriate books from the annotated bibliographies. References are numerous and broad-based to serve both parents looking for answers to individual questions and teachers and students involved in theory and research. The orientation of this book is topical rather than chronological. Major issues of infancy, as well as practical implications of infancy research, have been addressed. Among the many topics discussed are physical development, nutrition and feeding, the development of language abilities, the social development of the infant within the family, peer relations, play, and infant child care.

Occasionally research studies are mentioned. These have been used to illustrate infant functioning. Focus is on the concept illustrated rather than details of the research mentioned.

It is the hope of the authors that those people working with or caring for infants will find *Infancy* a handy and helpful reference. The finished product represents our joint contribution and our sincere dedication to the period of life called "infancy."

Deborah Lovitky Sheiman, Ed.D., on behalf of the authors:

Hannah Nuba-Scheffler, M.S.
Deborah Lovitky Sheiman, Ed.D.
Kathleen Pullan Watkins, Ed.D.

Infancy

INFANT PHYSICAL DEVELOPMENT

Deborah Lovitky Sheiman

Understanding the physical development of infants means understanding the developmental cycle of life from conception forward. Birth of the average 7-pound, 20-inch baby is but a waystop in an ongoing developmental process. During the nine months of prenatal growth, nature has taken the organism from the germinal stage to an embryo to a fetus.

During the germinal stage, from conception to movement, the organism is implanted in the wall of the mother's uterus. Location of cells within this structure determines their differentiation. One area will produce cells that group to create the embryonic disk from which a baby will grow. Other parts of the structure create the necessary life-sustaining systems, such as the placenta, which links the bloodstreams of the fetus and mother, passing nutrients and oxygen.

During the embryonic stage, from about two weeks post-fertilization to the beginning of the third month, major organs, limbs, and vital systems are differentiated. If this process occurs improperly, or not at all, the infant will emerge defective. It is during this period of major differentiation that the embryo is most vulnerable to toxin damage. Spontaneous abortion or miscarriage during the embryonic stage is common, usually occurring because developmental abnormalities render the embryo incapable of survival.

By 10 to 12 weeks after fertilization the embryo has begun to take on recognizably human characteristics. Though only about an inch long, large eyes and tongue and tooth buds are apparent on a large head. The heart is beating, and the stomach produces digestive juices while the kidneys filter blood. Arms, legs, fingers, and toes are beginning to emerge. All major organs, with the exception of the genitals, are identifiable.

The fetal stage begins around the third month of pregnancy. Appendages that were buds during the embryonic stage differentiate and develop. Networks of veins and muscle connections

appear. Reflexes evolve. Swallowing and urination emerge as
the functional capacity of the fetus multiplies. By six months
the fetus is viable, meaning that it is capable of surviving
outside of the womb. However, the infant is at high risk if
sophisticated and technological skills and equipment are not
available. In the last trimester of pregnancy the fetus must
ready itself for adaptation to the world outside the womb.
It gains weight and creates fat pads under the skin providing
for temperature insulation.

At birth the infant undertakes the life-supporting systems
that the mother had previously furnished. Taking nourishment
through the mouth now becomes the infant's function.

The passage from the womb to the outside world leaves most
infants temporarily with a withered and reddened appearance.
A white, cheeselike substance covers the skin and is easily
washed away. This served to protect the skin while the fetus
was surrounded by amniotic fluid. Newborns have small bodies
and limbs and large heads, the latter accounting for about a
quarter of their body size. Babylike features, such as large
round faces, big eyes, large foreheads, and round noses, elicit
adult feelings of nurturance and protection.

The minute-to-minute demeanor of the newborn is dependent
on state of arousal. This denotes the newborn's ability to
respond to the environment. Each state of arousal is charac-
terized by differences in respiration, muscle tone, motor activity, and alertness. Sleeping and wakefulness comprise the
infant's functional behavior. These two phases are subdivided
into separate states of arousal and are classified as sleep,
irregular sleep, periodic sleep, drowsiness, alert inactivity,
waking activity, and crying.

Infant survival and adaptability are facilitated by a
repertoire of reflexes or unlearned fixed responses that occur
as direct reaction to a specific stimulus. Three types of
reflexes aid early survival. These include reflexes such as
shivering, which helps maintain constant body temperature;
sucking, which promotes adequate nourishment; and reflexes
that help maintain regular breathing. For example, an adaptive response to suffocation is the head-turning reflex. Laying
the infant face down elicits a head turn to the side to facilitate breathing.

Reflexes provide a starting point for making contact with
the environment over the first weeks of life. As the baby
becomes more adaptive, reflexes begin to disappear. This is
attributable to cortical control mechanisms. Behavior turns
from involuntary to voluntary.

Infancy is a stage of rapid physical development as bones,
muscles, and nervous system mature. Increasingly, the infant's
body takes on childlike proportions. Physical development is

sequential, appearing in a head-to-"tail" sequence and near-to-far sequence from the center of the body outward. Therefore, the infant has control over the upper body and limbs before the lower body and limbs. Muscle groups such as those in the shoulders develop allowing arm use before muscles in the fingers develop contributing to small motor control. Another feature of physical development is the emergence of basic skills first. These grow more complex through practice, mastery, and integration with other basic skills.

Infants follow a common chronological, developmental pattern. By the beginning of the second month of life they can lift their heads high while lying on their stomachs. By the end of that same month rolling over and sitting propped up are seen. Gross motor development accelerates into the fifth month when babies master the skill of sitting alone and creeping. During the sixth month the coordination of arm and leg movements allow for crawling. The ability to stand appears around month 11 and walking at a year. The ability to walk changes baby's classification from infant to toddler. At this stage gait is a toddle from side to side. Short legs must be spread wide for stability, giving an unbalanced, toddling appearance.

During the second year of life toddlers learn to walk backwards (approximately 14 months), master steps (17 months), kick a ball (20 months), and run well (24 months).

Coexisting is the development of fine motor control. At approximately the sixth month most babies hold a toy until interest is lost and the muscles of the hand relax causing the toy to drop. By around the seventh month the art of letting go is mastered.

Focus now turns to the use of fingers for grasping. First attempts show the palm and the fourth and fifth fingers forming the grasp. This is followed by the center of the palm and middle fingers, or the side of the palm and index finger, producing a grasp. The skill is complete around 9 to 14 months when thumb and forefinger form a grasp.

Each of these skills requires considerable practice and refinement to achieve mastery. The norms given for each skill should be viewed cautiously. Norms are only averages. They are not universal and are subject to change. As noted, most American babies walk around one year. In the 1920s the norm was 15 months. Today, in the country of Uganda, most babies walk at 10 months. Variances in norms are due to different cultural patterns of baby care, standards of health, and the degree of adequate nutrition.

Norms are useful to highlight extremely slow development and risk of developmental problems. Happy, healthy, active infants who progress slightly faster or slower than the norms are normal babies with their own timetables. They are not necessarily any more or less capable than babies following the norms. Maturational level, environment, and individual desire for mastery affect development.

Physical development is a rapid progression of changes in size, shapes, and skills. Each level of advancement allows infants to become increasingly active in their environment. Examining growth gives insight into the development and integration of skills leading to the baby's sense of physical integrity.

BIBLIOGRAPHY

1. Annis, Linda Ferrill. *Child Before Birth*. Ithaca, N.Y.: Cornell University Press, 1978.

   In this book, Annis, a specialist in human growth and development, describes the normal stages of prenatal child development and analyzes possible harmful influences. Covered are genetic diseases of the infant, maternal malnutrition, the effects of the use of drugs, alcohol, and smoking plus the effects of the emotional state of the mother. The material covered will be especially helpful to counselors, social workers, nurses, nutritionists, and drug therapists, as well as pregnant women.

2. Barber, Lucy, and Herman Williams. *Your Baby's First Thirty Months*. Tucson, Ariz.: H.P. Books, 1981.

   Filled with practical suggestions for first-time parents, this book is written from a baby's point of view. Each chapter includes space for parents to record their own observations.

3. Belsky, Jay. *In the Beginning: Readings in Infancy*. New York: Columbia University Press, 1982.

   This volume is for parents and professionals interested in current literature and research in the field of pre- and postnatal development. There are also discussions on pre- and postnatal influences and emotional and cognitive development. The time period covered extends to the child's second year.

4. Bernath, Maja. *Parent's Book for Your Baby's First Year.*
   New York: Ballantine, 1983.

   Bernath provides a comprehensive guide for each stage of
   development of a child's first 12 months. In addition,
   such topics are covered as baby-sitting pools, support
   for working mothers, day-care alternatives, questions
   relating to routine check-ups, immunization, medical
   tests, recognizing illness in an infant, the medicine
   chest, and infant safety.

5. Bloom, Arthur, and L.S. James. *The Fetus and the Newborn.*
   New York: March of Dimes, 1981.

   This publication, one of an annual series of reviews
   on birth defects published by the March of Dimes, addresses
   birth defects in both the fetus and early infancy. It also
   covers such issues as genetic screening and counseling.

6. Bower, T.G.R. *A Primer of Infant Development.* San Francisco: Freeman, 1977.

   According to Bower, for many years infancy was "like the
   dark side of the moon." In the recent past there has been
   a surge of information that brings to light many aspects
   of infant development that previously were thought un-
   answerable. In this book the author summarizes available
   data and puts it into a context that would be useful to
   professionals and parents. Although there is no index,
   there is a useful bibliography.

7. Brazelton, T. Berry. *Infants and Mothers: Differences in
   Development,* rev. ed. New York: Delacorte/Seymour Lawrence, 1983.

   The author, a distinguished pediatrician, has incorporated
   in this revised edition, the latest research findings in
   infant development at the time of publication. In addition, he considers the challenges that face new parents
   today more than in previous generations. The role of the
   father and pressures on working mothers are sensitively
   discussed. Dr. Brazelton, a strong advocate for babies,
   hopes that this book will serve to increase the sense of
   competence and pleasure in new parents so that they can
   enjoy their parenthood and transfer these feelings to the
   new infant.

8. Brunner, Jerome. *Human Growth and Development.* *See*
   Chapter 4, item 171.

9. Diagram Group. *Child's Body.* New York: Bantam, 1979.

   This book containing numerous charts and diagrams is
   designed to provide clear explanations of every aspect
   of the body's functioning, care, and development. Chapters include discussion of anatomy and physiology, child
   development, illness and disease, food and exercise, and
   first aid. The information is comprehensive, and statis-
   tics are offered in interesting ways. According to the
   authors, material in this book was presented to a team
   of practicing pediatricians and child-care experts for
   their advice and review. The detailed table of contents
   and good index help make the book easy to use.

10. Feldman, George B., with Anne Felshman. *A Complete Hand-
    book of Pregnancy.* New York: Putnam, 1984.

    An unusual format allows for a systematic tracing of
    the pregnant mother's progress as well as that of the
    developing baby. The appendices include lists of organi-
    zations concerned with pregnancy, childbirth, and children.

11. Flanagan, Geraldine. *The First Nine Months of Life.*
    New York: Simon & Schuster, 1982.

    With the help of illustrations and photographs, the
    author describes every stage of embryonic growth. The
    goal is to assist the reader to gain increased understand-
    ing of human development, as well as to learn to appre-
    ciate the beauty of the birth experience.

12. Frank, Lawrence Kelso. *On the Importance of Infancy.*
    New York: Random House, 1966.

    The focus of this dated, but interesting, volume is on
    the growing realization of infancy as a critical stage
    in human development. In order to provide greater under-
    standing of this period in human development, Frank dis-
    cusses research in the field. However, his book is not
    meant as a systematic review of the literature on infancy
    at that time.

13. Gesell, Arnold, et al. *Infant and Child in the Culture
    of Today: The Guidance of Development in Home and
    Nursery School,* rev. ed. New York: Harper & Row, 1974.

    A classic in the field of child care, this volume is
    based on years of systematic research at the Gesell In-
    stitute of Child Development. In addition to the research
    findings, the focus is mainly on the growth characteris-
    tics of the infant and child. Written in clear and simple
    language, the text is directed at both parents and pro-
    fessionals.

14. Johnson & Johnson Baby Products Company. *The First Wondrous Year: You and Your Baby*. *See* Chapter 7, item 300.

15. Koch, Jaroslav. *Total Baby Development*. New York: Wyden, 1976.

    A baby exercise book with a difference, the focus is on achieving the infant's total potential through physical movement and goal-oriented activity. Drawings illustrate the step-by-step program outlined.

16. Leach, Penelope. *Babyhood*, 2nd ed. New York: Knopf, 1983.

    This book describes babyhood, stage by stage. A review of child development during the first two years, it is written for parents as well as professionals who work with babies and their parents. Each skill discussed is separated into time periods so that the reader can pick a certain age and read a chapter pertaining to each period to understand the development of a skill. The author provides the reader with an overview of infant development, a "feel for what it is like to be a parent," and a report on research studies and sources of further information. The bibliography has both American and European references.

17. Leach, Penelope. *Your Baby and Child: From Birth to Age Five*. New York: Knopf, 1978.

    Leach has written a very comprehensive and very readable book on the development of the child from age one to five. The book is sectioned by age, but the encyclopedic index is arranged alphabetically. The format makes it easy to look things up in a hurry. Many illustrations supplement the text.

18. Leavenworth, Carol, et al. *Family Living*. *See* Chapter 7, item 308.

19. Levy, Janine. *The Baby Exercise Book: The First Fifteen Months*. New York: Pantheon, 1975.

    This is a detailed, pictorial guide for parents in how to aid an infant's growth by exercising the infant, using his natural movements. Dr. Levy considers four stages of the child's motor development: (1) birth to three months, (2) three to six months, (3) six to twelve months, and (4) nine to fifteen months.

20. McCall, Robert B. *Infants: The New Knowledge.* *See* Chapter 4, item 183.

21. Moore, Shirley G., and Catherine R. Cooper, eds. *The Young Child.* Reviews of Research, Vol. 3. *See* Chapter 3, item 138.

22. Pomeranz, Virginia, and Dodie Schwartz. *From One to Two: Your Baby's Second Year.* New York: New American Library, 1984.

    The authors survey a child's physical and social development in the second year. They consider such topics as language acquisition, toilet training, first aid, as well as other relevant topics for the child of this age period. However, this book is not an extensive work. Parents looking for more detailed information would probably do better with another source.

23. Queenan, J. *A New Life: Pregnancy, Birth and Your Child's First Year.* *See* Chapter 7, item 322.

24. Richards, M. *Infancy: World of the Newborn.* *See* Chapter 3, item 143.

25. Ridenour, R. *Motor Development: Issues--Application.* Princeton, N.J.: Princeton Book, 1978.

    This well-written book talks about current issues in the study of motor development of young children. It is divided into three sections. The first offers a brief discussion of growth and motor development. The second section covers issues in motor development, such as infant motor development programs and sex differences. The third section considers applications of theory, such as play-space design, development motor task analysis, and assessment of motor development. This would be an excellent book for gym teachers, classroom teachers, nurses, and physical therapists. There are two appendices: one offers suggestions for locating relevant literature and the other discusses the setting up of a motor development laboratory. Ridenour also presents an impressive bibliography.

26. Scheffler, Hannah Nuba (ed.). *Resources for Early Childhood: An Annotated Bibliography and Guide for Educators, Librarians, Health Care Professionals, and Parents.* *See* Chapter 7, item 327.

27. Smart, Mollie S., and Russell C. Smart. *Infants: Development and Relationships. See* Chapter 3, item 153.

28. Smith, Lendon H. *The Encyclopedia of Baby and Child Care. See* Chapter 2, item 85.

29. Spock, Benjamin. *Baby and Child Care.* New York: Pocket Books, 1981.

This classic volume on all aspects of child rearing is written by one of the most widely respected authorities on the subject. In 1985 in collaboration with Dr. Michael B. Rothenberg, he published *Dr. Spock's Baby and Child Care* which supplements his original classic. *See* Chapter 7, item 332.

30. Stone, L. Joseph, Henrietta T. Smith, and Lois B. Murphy, eds. *The Competent Infant: Research and Commentary. See* Chapter 4, item 204.

31. White, B. *The First Three Years of Life.* New York: Avon, 1975.

White offers "up-to-date information about how you can help your child acquire a solid foundation for full development." He refers to the work of Piaget, Maslow, Murphy, and Hunt and presents the normal development patterns of the very young child and applications of early child-rearing principles. This book is intended for parents and child-care workers. For each of the seven phases of the first three years, White reviews general behavior of the child, the educational development, recommended practices, and practices not recommended. Several tables are included as are some drawings.

2

NUTRITION AND HEALTH CONCERNS IN INFANCY

Deborah Lovitky Sheiman

"Whatever mother eats, fetus eats." A healthy newborn is dependent on mother's diet throughout pregnancy. Mother's calorie consumption increases by 10 to 20 percent to assure fetal growth. During this period protein needs rise 50 percent and calcium, phosphorus, and vitamin C demands are doubled. What happens to the developing fetus when the mother's diet provides inadequate nutrition? Directly, malnourishment increases risk of low birth weight, stillbirth, and infant mortality. Indirectly, poor maternal nourishment means high susceptibility to disease. Seriously ill mothers can produce sick or defective infants.

Maternal malnutrition during the last trimester of pregnancy can be especially harmful to fetal brain development. A malnourished fetus has a decreased number of brain cells. There are fewer connective links between nerve cells in the brain and slower development of sheathing around nerves. If nutritional deficits are rectified and sustained during the early months of life, the negative effects of malnutrition can be overcome. However, inadequate or improper nutrition that continues for the first year or two can result in permanent consequences.

The early years of life are a time for establishing sound dietary practices. The infant's body has a small storehouse of nutrients and is easily affected by daily intake. Normal weight gain averages two pounds per month for the first three months and thereafter one pound per month for nine months. Calorie and nutrient requirements are directly related to infant growth rate.

During the first year of life most calories and nutrients are supplied through milk. Whether the milk is obtained from mother's breast or properly prepared commercial formula is an individual decision. The American Academy of Pediatrics recommends nursing as the optimal method of feeding.

Nursing can be advantageous to the mother. Regardless of the total weight gained during pregnancy, around ten pounds are accumulated fat. Nursing helps to use up these extra calories. Mothers who nurse return to their normal weight sooner than nonnursing mothers, who must diet to lose the extra pounds. Breast feeding promotes the quick return of the uterus to its original size and inhibits ovulation. Additionally, it is quick and convenient. There is no need for bottles or warming milk. Mother's lactation is naturally adapted to baby's sucking. The more baby sucks, the more milk produced.

The advantages for baby are even greater. Mother's milk is specific to the needs of the human infant. Commercial formulas cannot reproduce the nutritional values of human milk. There are differences in the amount and form of protein, and human milk contains 50 percent more lactose and 20 percent more fat than the harder-to-digest cow's milk.

Breast milk protects against, and promotes baby's resistance to, infection. Mother's body produces antibodies that combat harmful bacteria. These antibodies are transmitted to baby at a time when baby's body is too immature to produce its own antibodies. Breast milk also fosters growth of intestinal bacteria that inhibits development of harmful organisms. A nursed baby is more active, has more neonatal weight gain, and is less likely to become obese.

Nursing mothers must carefully choose their diet. Restraint from alcohol, nicotine, drugs, and foods contaminated with industrial pollutants is necessary.

Mothers who cannot, or who choose not, to nurse can still raise happy, healthy infants on formula. The psychological aspects of feeding that promote attachment can occur with breast or bottle feeding. Feeding time is an important time for mother/child interaction. Holding baby close, making eye contact, playing and talking to baby during feedings facilitate optimal feelings of closeness and love.

Mothers should be alert to the problem of allowing older infants to fall asleep while sucking on the breast or bottle. The natural sugars in mother's milk and formula leave a residue in the mouth and on the teeth that promotes decay. Undiscovered decay can cause discomfort, infection, and damage to permanent teeth developing above baby teeth. Children's dentists recommend that nursed babies be removed from the breast before falling asleep. Formula-fed babies should be given a diluted mixture of 85 percent water and 15 percent milk, gradually cut down to all water, immediately before sleep occurs.

Though mother's milk or formula is adequate to sustain the initial needs of the infant, the introduction of solid foods is needed around four to six months. This begins the gradual

process of weaning. Fortified cereals are first introduced.
These are followed by fruits, vegetables, and meats.
   Only one new food should be added at a time. No other
new food is given for several days. The interval between
food introductions is necessary to determine baby's ability
to tolerate each new product. Foods such as eggs, wheat, and
whole milk are frequently connected to allergies. Even milk-
based infant formulas can cause allergies. In these cases
alternative soy products are substituted. The infant's level
of antibodies necessary to neutralize allergic substances is
not built up until around seven months. Withholding of commonly allergic foods until seven to nine months can reduce
the chance of allergy. Parents should be alerted to allergic
reactions, particularly if there is an allergic history in the
family.
   Milk volume should be reduced when solids are introduced.
Milk plus solids should equal the infant's total nutritional
requirements. Encouraging baby to finish all formula and
solids can lead to overfeeding.
   Understanding the order of feeding development can help
caregivers to have appropriate expectations and a positive
experience at baby's mealtime. From birth to two months,
feeding is a reflexive process. Baby has little control of
head, lips, and tongue. Milk is commonly lost from the mouth,
though the ability to swallow is adequate. By the end of the
third month, feeding is no longer reflexive and control is
continually improving.
   Baby begins to feed with lips closed by four to six months.
Coordination of head, lips, and tongue has improved. The
volume of liquid lost in feeding is greatly reduced, though
spoon feeding can still be a problem. Six to eight months
brings major feeding developments. Baby is able to sit and
hold the bottle independently. Many babies begin to drink
from a cup at this age; however, parents should expect liquid
loss since baby is just learning to coordinate lips, tongue,
and cup.
   From eight to ten months, coordination of head and mouth
improves, resulting in decreased spilling from spoon or cup.
Baby begins a biting or munching response to food that leads
to finger-feeding skills at ten to twelve months. The baby
views food as enjoyable. Playing with food should be expected.
Holding the cup with two hands leads to baby's independence--
and spilling.
   During the child's second year of life, feeding skills
become coordinated and established. The toddler is able to
eat most table foods, cut into small, chewable pieces and
served in toddler-sized portions. Foods such as popcorn,
nuts, and hard candies should be avoided until age five.

Small, hard foods can become lodged in the windpipe, resulting
in choking and suffocation.

During the second and third years of life, a child develops a sense of independence. This can be exhibited through
food refusals. At this stage, today's favorite food can become tomorrow's rejected food. Picky and erratic eating habits
are common. Rejected foods can be presented in a different
manner and served again a few days later. The quantity of
food consumed depends on the child's daily activity level and
physical and emotional stress. A child is likely to eat less
if in a strange or new surrounding or with unfamiliar people.
Parents should not worry if their child goes through a period
of erratic eating. Physiologist Walter B. Cannon notes that
we eat what our body requires nutritionally: "Body wisdom
sensitizes us to the nutrients needed by our body, so we can
adapt intake accordingly."

Should children who eat erratically take vitamins? If a
child is a poor eater and not receiving adequate nutrition, a
parent might feel more comfortable dispensing a one-a-day
multiple vitamin with iron. However, when a child's appetite
is adequate and diet is well-balanced, there is little need
for vitamins. Vitamin deficiency is uncommon in the United
States since a large percentage of commercially prepared food
products are nutrient-fortified. High doses of vitamins are,
at best, controversial and, at worst, harmful to a child.
The range between requirement and toxicity is narrow for some
vitamins. Consultation with the pediatrician is recommended
before any vitamin prophylaxis or therapy is begun.

Obesity can also become a problem during infancy. Overfeeding a baby an extra 100-calorie-a-day bottle can produce
a too heavy baby by year's end. A heavy baby is less active,
and inactive babies become heavier.

A parent's genetic inheritance affects the child's risk
for obesity. If both parents are overweight, it is likely
that the child will follow suit. It is also likely that slim
parents will have slim children. Genetic inheritance, plus a
tendency to eat the wrong foods or overfeed, increases the
child's risk of obesity.

During the first two years of life, fat cell development
is rapid. Overfeeding can cause an abnormally high number of
fat cells in the body, or hypertrophic obesity, in which fat
cells are greatly enlarged but normal in number. The best
defense against obesity in childhood is a caring parent who
takes cues from the child as to mealtime completion. Making
baby empty the bottle or eating until the plate is clean may
be harmful. When children lose interest in their food, they
are no longer hungry. Healthy diet, adequate exercise, and
eating only until satisfied can protect the child from the
lifelong problem of obesity.

Along with sound dietary practices, baby medical checkups promote well-being. Checkups are done monthly for the first six months, then again at nine months and one year. During the second and third years of life, they are biannual, until the age of three when yearly visits are adequate. Parents should not hesitate to call or visit the pediatrician more frequently if they have health, nutritional, or developmental concerns.

Alert parents can quickly respond to the telltale signs of illness with a call to the doctor. Some of these warning signals are chills and fever, persistent coughing and sneezing, bodily pain, bowel or urination irregularities, change in pallor, and change in temperament and/or behavior.

Problems such as fever, diarrhea, vomiting, and colds are experienced by all children at some point in time. A reference copy of a children's health-care manual can give practical advice and is a must for every home with children. A sick child needs additional bed rest or quiet time, plus lots of tender loving care. A child may show fear and anxiety over illness and the accompanying unpleasant sensations never before experienced.

Prepare children over 18 months for visits to doctors and medical procedures. Honest, simple explanation of what will occur will ease the child's anxiety. Under 18 months of age, a baby or toddler should be distracted during an unpleasant procedure. Hold and talk to the child as much as possible. The security of a loving parent while in a strange and sometimes painful environment of a doctor's office or hospital is needed.

Normal bowel and bladder control are important health issues during toddlerhood. Toilet training is most successful around age two to three years. By this time the child is aware of physiological cues and is able to maintain sphincter control. The toddler is able to get to the toilet and remove easy-to-pull-down clothing, take the correct position on the toilet, and then release control. This sequence of events takes an intellectual ability to understand the process, a linguistic ability to communicate the process, and a physiological ability to control the muscles. Attempting toilet training before the child has these abilities means training the parent rather than the child. Bladder control comes before bowel control, and daytime control comes before nighttime control. Boys are slightly slower to train than are girls.

Babies and toddlers are healthier today than ever before. Their parents are better informed concerning developmental, health, and nutritional issues. Greater emphasis on prevention and promotion of well-being means healthier babies for today and the future.

BIBLIOGRAPHY

32. Adebonjo, Festus, and Eleanor Sherman, with Linda Jones.
     How Baby Grows. New York: Arbor House, 1985.

     This book is designed to lessen the guesswork involved
     in feeding infants. It is particularly illuminating in
     regard to vitamin and mineral requirements for infants.

33. Applegate, Kay. *The Little Book of Baby Foods.* Santa
     Fe, N.M.: Lightning Tree, 1978.

     The author details the preparation of baby foods from
     formulas to cereals to meat substitutes. This basic
     informative paperback is aimed at new parents. It is
     printed in English and Spanish.

34. Bell, David. *A Time to Be Born.* New York: Morrow, 1975.

     Written by a neonatologist, this book provides insight
     into the workings of a modern intensive-care nursery.
     The daily struggles and sacrifices of physicians and
     nurses, as well as the emotional pain of parents with
     sick newborns, is vividly described.

35. *Better Homes and Gardens* Editors. *Better Homes and
     Gardens New Baby Book.* New York: Bantam, 1980.

     Comprehensive and detailed, this book covers all as-
     pects of pregnancy, childbirth, and child care. There
     are many charts throughout the volume that the reader
     will find very helpful.

36. Brace, Edward R. *The Pediatric Guide to Drugs and Vita-
     mins.* New York: Dell, 1982.

     Brace has written a general reference book for parents
     and other interested adults looking for clear and concise
     information on drugs physicians prescribe for infants and
     young children, as well as the freely available over-the-
     counter drugs. Alphabetically arranged, over 150 drugs
     are listed, each with detailed information about the
     generic name, purpose, dosage for children, precautions
     to be aware of, and possible side effects.

37. Brewer, Gail, and Janice P. Greene. *Right from the Start:
     Meeting the Challenges of Mothering Your Unborn Baby.*
     Emmaus, Pa.: Rodale, 1981.

     This book provides the expectant parents with informa-
     tion about pregnancy, medical care, and early infant

care. Emphasis is on nutrition. The authors tend to be
critical of the medical profession and traditional hospital care.

38. Castle, Sue. *The Complete New Guide to Preparing Baby
    Foods at Home.* Garden City, N.Y.: Doubleday, 1981.

    Castle provides a wealth of nutrition information and
    consumer guidelines about foods for the baby, as well as
    helpful hints on storing foods, reading labels correctly,
    and what kitchen equipment works best in baby food
    preparation. In addition, she lists the nutritive
    values of various foods.

39. Coffin, Lewis A. *Children's Nutrition: A Consumer's
    Guide.* Santa Barbara, Calif.: Capra Press, 1984.

    Too many parents still feed their children the way
    they were fed when they were little. The author, a prac-
    ticing pediatrician and father of four, strongly asserts
    that "traditions are the perpetrators of horrendous
    dietary practices which we must toss from our lives...."
    Topics discussed include the hungry baby syndrome, the
    fat child, and the vegetarian baby. There is a guide
    for feeding the baby.

40. Cohen, Jean-Pierre. *Childhood: The First Six Years.*
    Englewood Cliffs, N.J.: Prentice-Hall, 1983.

    Emphasis is on the important role a parent plays in a
    child's total development. Cohen discusses breast feed-
    ing, nutrition, toilet learning, and child-rearing ques-
    tions. He includes a medical reference guide for child-
    hood illnesses, covering the gamut from minor to serious
    ailments.

41. Cohen, Jean-Pierre, and Roger Goirand. *Your Baby: Preg-
    nancy, Delivery, and Infant Care.* Englewood Cliffs,
    N.J.: Prentice-Hall, 1982.

    The authors--one a pediatrician, the other a specialist
    in obstetrics and gynecology--combine their expertise and
    experience in this guide to perinatal care. From amnio-
    centesis to x-ray, this book, translated from the French,
    Mon bébé, brings a fresh, relevant approach to the con-
    nected topics of pregnancy, delivery, and child care.

42. Collipp, Platon J. *Childhood Obesity,* 2nd ed. Littleton,
    Mass.: Wright-PGS, 1980.

    Collipp has written a well-balanced discussion of the
    factors involved in childhood obesity. Obesity accompany-

ing special needs (the Klinefelter syndrome) is differentiated from simple obesity. The book is for the health-
care and/or nutrition professional interested in theoretical and clinical data.

43. *Commonsense Guide to Birth and Babies, The.* By the
      Editors of Time-Life Books. New York: Holt, Rinehart
      and Winston, 1985.

      This is a comprehensive handbook about conception,
      pregnancy, birth, and child care for first-time parents.
      Included are illustrated instructions on nursing, bathing,
      and diapering the baby. Other features are guidelines
      for administering medication and a pharamcological chart
      explaining drugs and their effects.

44. *Consumer Guide*, Editors of. *The Complete Baby Book.*
      See Chapter 7, item 282.

45. Diagram Group. *Child's Body*. *See* Chapter 1, item 9.

46. Endres, Jeanette, and Robert E. Rockwell. *Food, Nutrition
      and the Young Child*. St. Louis, Mo.: Mosby, 1980.

      Basic concepts for nutrition are explained along with
      the food needs of young children from birth to age five.
      Mental and physical development of the child is discussed
      in connection with good nutrition. It is useful for
      parents and food service personnel, and preschool teachers.
      The latter will find food-related activities that can be
      incorporated into their curriculum. The Index of Nu-
      tritional Quality, which is included, is explained and
      examples of its application given.

47. Ewy, Donna, and Rodger Ewy. *Guide to Parenting: You and
      Your Newborn*. New York: Dutton, 1981.

      Focusing on the infant's first six weeks of life, the
      authors deal with such issues as daily infant care,
      health, and nutrition, as well as shared parenting and
      changing parental roles. Information is also given on
      how to select a pediatrician and how to choose appropriate
      nursery equipment.

48. Farran, Christopher. *Infant Colic: What It Is and What
      You Can Do About It*. New York: Scribner, 1984.

      The single best feature of infant colic is that every
      colicky baby will eventually outgrow the condition.
      Parents struggling to survive this trying period will

find this a useful resource. Given are sound suggestions for soothing the baby, as well as ways for the parents to cope with the seemingly endless crying of an otherwise healthy child.

49. Fried, Peter A. *Pregnancy and Life-Style Habits*. New York: Beaufort, 1983.

     Today's pregnant woman is conscious of the effects various substances such as alcohol, caffeine, nicotine, marijuana and other thought-altering drugs may have on the unborn infant. Less is understood about the use of prescribed and nonprescription drugs--including vitamin supplements, antacids, over-the-counter painkillers, etc. This book will help the mother-to-be make informed decisions about such substances.

50. Gansberg, Judith, and Arthur P. Mostel. *The Second Nine Months: The Sexual and Emotional Concerns of the New Mother*. *See* Chapter 7, item 292.

51. Goldsmith, Robert H. *Nutrition and Learning*. Bloomington, Ind.: Phi Delta Kappa, 1980.

     The relationship of nutrition to cognitive and motor development is examined in this small volume from the Phi Delta Kappa Educational Foundation. Specific nutritionally related learning problems are discussed. Positive preventive nutrition education is considered from the viewpoint of the schools.

52. Gots, Ronald, and Barbara Gots. *Caring for Your Unborn Child*. New York: Bantam, 1979.

     Detailed information is provided on the detrimental effect that even the simplest drugs can have on a baby's development.

53. Goulart, Frances Sheridan. *Beyond Baby Fat: Weight-Loss Plans for Children and Teenagers*. New York: McGraw-Hill, 1985.

     Children get fat for a variety of reasons. A properly balanced diet right from the start has a positive impact. The author makes a strong case for parental intervention, giving guidelines for combating overweight from pregnancy through adolescence.

54. Grams, Marilyn. *Breastfeeding Success for Working Mothers*. Carson City, Nev.: National Capital Resources, 1985.

Grams details practical guidelines for the working mother that help in finding ways to breast feed successfully while on the job.

55. Haessler, Herbert A. *How to Make Sure Your Baby Is Well--and Stays That Way. The First Guide to Over 400 Medical Tests and Treatments You Can Do at Home to Check Your Baby's Daily Health and Growth.* New York: Rawson, 1984.

"Confidence in dealing with new babies and young children comes from two sources--knowledge and experience." The author, a pediatrician, sets out to help parents tune into their new baby's health in a confident manner by showing how to detect problems early and "nip illness in the bud."

56. Hess, Mary A., and Anne E. Hunt. *Pickles and Ice Cream: The Complete Guide to Nutrition During Pregnancy.* New York: Dell, 1984.

Sprinkled with wit and humor, this book discusses weight gain and physiological changes that occur during pregnancy. The importance of good nutrition is explained in detail. How to eat well in restaurants and fast food places is also discussed.

57. Jones, Sandy. *Crying Baby, Sleepless Nights: How to Overcome Baby's Sleep Problems--And Get Some Sleep Yourself.* New York: Warner Books, 1983.

Here is a guide, designed to be helpful to parents as well as professionals who are interested in the latest research about the causes of an infant's crying. Included is a directory of support groups for parents, information on finding the right pediatrician, and many suggestions on how best to handle a variety of everyday situations--situations that can become serious problems without the proper answers.

58. Kitzinger, Sheila. *The Experience of Breastfeeding.* New York: Penguin, 1980.

This book, by a childbirth educator and social anthropologist, is not a how-to book but a fascinating overview of breast-feeding. Kitzinger is an obvious proponent of nursing. Throughout she identifies the importance of the whole family relationship. There is an extensive review of the literature, presented in a scholarly manner and intermingled with child development knowledge. The text distinguishes between "nutritional" and "comfort" suckling.

59. Krause, Marie V., and Kathleen Mahan. *Food Nutrition and Diet Therapy: A Textbook of Nutritional Care*, 7th ed. Philadelphia: Saunders, 1984.

The authors have compiled a concise and complete reference. Nutrition throughout the life cycle is discussed with primary consideration given to pregnancy, infancy, and childhood through adolescence. There is an excellent chapter on the nutritional management of health problems during infancy and childhood. Although the text is geared to the professional, it does contain valuable information for all readers.

60. La Leche League International. *The Womanly Art of Breast-feeding*. Franklin Park, Ill.: The League, 1983.

First published in 1958, this book is considered a "classic," if not the bible, of breast-feeding advice and support. The mother-to-be will learn what preparations to make for nursing, the adjustments to be made after birth, and how to cope with family reactions. In addition, there is guidance for the nursing mother in special circumstances, such as Cesarean birth, and the role of the father is stressed.

61. Lansky, Vicki. *Feed Me! I'm Yours*. New York: Bantam, 1981.

This popular, easy-to-read book is available only in paperback. The author's approach is positive, innovative, and fun. Included are recipes, new ideas on home preparation of baby foods, and helpful hints on making mealtime enjoyable for both mother and baby.

62. Lawrence, Ruth A. *Breast-Feeding: A Guide for the Medical Profession*. St. Louis: Mosby, 1980.

The author examines topics such as dietary influence during lactation, the effect of maternal intake of drugs on breast milk, and the pros and cons of breast feeding. Special consideration is given to the subject of weaning. Although intended for the medical profession, the book furnishes useful information for the lay reader.

63. Leach, Penelope. *Your Baby and Child: From Birth to Age Five. See* Chapter 1, item 17.

64. Lief, Nina R., with Mary Ellen Fahs, ed. *The First Year of Life: A Guide for Parents.* See Chapter 3, item 132.

65. McCall, Robert B. *Infants: The New Knowledge.* See Chapter 4, item 183.

66. MacMahon, Alice T. *All About Childbirth: A Manual for Perpared Childbirth.* Maitland, Fla.: Family Publications, 1983.

    As the title promises, this book is designed to be used as a childbirth education manual. The value and importance of informed preparation is the main message of this excellent manual. In addition to giving the reader as much information as possible on the various methods of childbirth, there are many practical tips on infant care and development, as well as on dieting, exercises for the mother-to-be, sexuality, and hospital and doctor interaction.

67. McWilliams, Margaret. *Nutrition for the Growing Years,* 3rd ed. New York: Wiley, 1980.

    McWilliams considers nutrition from a theoretical yet practical standpoint. In one chapter there is a sound scientific discussion of the interrelationship of nutrition to cognitive development. The role of childhood diet in preventative and maintenance health care is examined. Attention is given to the effects of adequate and inadequate nutrition on the developmental stages of infancy and childhood.

68. Marzollo, Jean, comp. *9 Months, 1 Day, 1 Year: A Guide to Pregnancy, Birth and Babycare.* See Chapter 7, item 312.

69. Maynard, Leslie-Jane. *When Your Child Is Overweight.* St. Meirnard, Ind.: Abbey, 1980.

    Practical advice is offered to parents of overweight children. Suggestions on overcoming the unescapable obstacles and impasses of children's weight control are discussed, as are the myths about obesity and grocery shopping tips.

70. *Mayo Clinic Diet Manual: A Handbook of Dietary Practices,* 5th ed. Mayo Clinic Dietetic Staff. Philadelphia: Saunders, 1981.

The dietary management information in this manual is
for the well-informed parent or clinician who is planning
a special diet for the allergic child or child with
health and/or metabolic problems. Specific information
is given to tailoring diets to the needs of the individual.
In addition, there is a resource-filled chapter on pregnancy and lactation that includes special considerations
of the adolescent and diabetic mother-to-be.

71. Meyer, Tamara. *Help Your Baby Build a Healthy Body: A
    New Exercise and Massage Program for the First Five
    Formative Years.* New York: Crown, 1984.

    All parents will find helpful guidelines on how to en-
    hance and encourage their child's motor development.

72. Natow, Annette, and Jo-Ann Heslin. *No-Nonsense Nutrition
    for Kids.* New York: McGraw-Hill, 1985.

    The authors offer sound, useful, and relevant informa-
    tion about nutrition for young children. Their discussion
    ranges from breast and bottle feeding to allergies to
    kid-tested recipes.

73. Norwood, Christopher. *At Highest Risk: Environmental
    Hazards to Young and Unborn Children.* New York: McGraw-
    Hill, 1980.

    Norwood describes the many potential risks posed to the
    unborn and young child by the environment, including
    genetic defects and developmental problems resulting from
    chemical toxins, drugs, x-rays, and even certain kinds of
    light bulbs.

74. Pantell, Robert H., James F. Fries, and Donald M. Vickery.
    *Taking Care of Your Child: A Parent's Guide to Medical
    Care,* rev. ed. Reading, Mass.: Addison-Wesley, 1984.

    The authors present detailed, step-by-step instructions
    pertaining to all aspects of home care for children.
    There are helpful "decision-making charts" that parents
    can use in deciding when to call the doctor or when the
    problem can be handled with home care. Another unique
    feature is the "Home Pharmacy" chapter that discusses a
    number of medicines for treating common symptoms.

75. Peavy, Linda S., and Andrea L. Paginkopt. *Grow Healthy
    Kids!: A Parents Guide to Sound Nutrition from Birth
    through Teens.* New York: Grosset & Dunlap, 1980.

A complete reference guide, this paperback presents useful ideas for encouraging sound eating habits in children. It deals with common concerns of mothers--breast vs. bottle feeding, effect(s) of diet on hyperactivity and other behavior problems, preventing iron deficiency anemia, obesity, and feeding a child with allergies. Helpful information on nutrition exchanges for specific diets, along with calorie tables, height and weight charts, and a bibliography are included.

76. Pennington, Jean, and Helen Church. *Bowes and Church's Food Values of Portions Commonly Used*, 13th ed. Philadelphia: Lippincott, 1980.

This is a quick resource for nutrient data. A cross-sampling of foods consumed by the general public is included. Listings describe the nutritive value of items from fast foods to baby formulas. Numerous tables and charts are presented. It is a handy, accurate reference guide.

77. Pipes, Peggy. *Nutrition in Infancy and Childhood*, 3rd ed. St. Louis: Mosby, 1984.

This comprehensive guide to all aspects of child nutrition has language that is somewhat technical yet easy to read. Nutrition is considered in relation to growth and development, feeding behaviors, and related problems. Information on vegetarian diets is included. Contributing authors provide practical experiences along with nutrition information. Nutritionists frequently recommend the volume as a "best-all-around" source.

78. Queenan, J. *A New Life: Pregnancy, Birth and Your Child's First Year. See* Chapter 7, item 322.

79. Regnier, Susan L. *You and Me, Baby: A Prenatal, Postpartum, and Infant Exercise Book*. Deephaven, Minn.: Meadowbrook Books, 1983.

Called "The Official YMCA Guide," these exercise routines were developed to be used in fitness classes in YMCA's around the country. Chapters touch on prenatal concerns and nutrition, as well as give instructions on how to monitor the heart and pulse rate during the workout. All the prenatal, postpartum and infant exercise programs are supplemented by photographs that make the steps easy to follow.

80. Richards, M. *Infancy: World of the Newborn. See* Chapter 3, item 143.

81. Salk, Leo. *Your Child's First Year. See* Chapter 3, item 148.

82. Scarpa, Joannis, and Helen Keifer. *Sourcebook on Food and Nutrition*, 2nd ed. Chicago: Marquis Academic Media, 1980.

    In this excellent resource publication the subjects covered include food fads, special diets, product labeling, vitamin myths, and food additives. A chapter is dedicated to the relationship of nutrition to the life cycle. Discussion of nutrition in fetal development and infancy is incorporated. The critical review of elimination diets should be read by any parents considering such therapy for their child.

83. Scheffler, Hannah Nuba, ed. *Resources for Early Childhood: An Annotated Bibliography and Guide for Educators, Librarians, Health Care Professionals, and Parents. See* Chapter 7, item 327.

84. Slattery, Jill, Gayle Angus Pearson, and Carolyn Talley Torre. *Maternal and Child Nutrition.* New York: Appleton-Century-Crofts, 1979.

    This excellent reference covers nutrition during pregnancy to nutrition in adolescence. Issues such as skim milk versus whole milk for the toddler and formula versus milk during late infancy are discussed. Attention is given to nutritional dysfunction and common food-related problems.

85. Smith, Lendon H. *The Encyclopedia of Baby and Child Care.* New York: Warner Books, 1980.

    This is an everything-you-need-to-know reference book, alphabetically arranged and cross-indexed. Part one covers emergencies, first aid and poisonings, allergies, drugs, and medicine. Part two discusses the anatomy and development of the newborn--skin, bones, muscles, circulatory system, etc. The author makes it clear that this book should not substitute for the family physician or pediatrician but can help one gain insight into how the child's body operates, how the child grows and develops, and how care and feeding affect health and behavior.

86. Smith, Lendon H. *Feed Your Kids Right.* New York: Dell, 1982.

Dr. Smith is well known to many parents as the Children's Doctor from his frequent appearances on television. He approaches his book with the philosophy that proper nutrition can prevent or forestall illness and help to maintain optimal health. This book contains a complete reference to the vitamins and minerals necessary for child growth and development.

87. Smith, Lendon H. *Foods for Healthy Kids.* New York: Berkley, 1982.

In his own style, Dr. Smith advises parents on the prevention, treatment, and cure of physical and behavioral problems that have relevance to diet--sleep disturbances, allergies, mood swings and hyperactivity. Each recipe lists the amounts of protein, calcium, vitamins, etc. Resource lists are included for free and inexpensive information and materials. There is a useful bibliography on this subject matter.

88. Spock, Benjamin. *Baby and Child Care.* See Chapter 1, item 29.

89. Spock, Benjamin, and M. Lowenberg. *Feeding Your Baby and Child.* Boston: Little, Brown, 1955.

Dr. Spock discusses diet during infancy and childhood. He provides information on the introduction of solid foods, formulas, and vitamin supplements. Dietary aspects of caring for a sick child are considered. The format of this early Spock publication is similar to that in his well-known *Baby and Child Care.*

90. Spock, Benjamin, and Michael B. Rothenberg. *Dr. Spock's Baby and Child Care.* See Chapter 7, item 332.

91. Stoutt, Glenn R., Jr. *The First Month of Life: A Parent's Guide to Care of the Newborn.* New York: New American Library, 1981.

This parenting guide provides answers new parents need during the first few weeks of their baby's life. Stoutt, a pediatrician, offers advice on breast feeding, formulas, solid foods, and colic. He discusses parent-infant bonding and other topics in an easy-to-read common-sense approach. The first half of the book deals with the practical physical care of the baby, such as feeding, bathing, clothing, car safety, etc. The second half concerns developing proper attitudes and feelings toward the baby to lead to a healthy parent-child relationship.

92. Thomas, Linda. *Caring and Cooking for the Allergic Child*. New York: Sterling, 1980.

In this excellent resource book for the mother of a child with malabsorption syndrome or allergies, Thomas offers advice on which recipes can be used for allergic children and how to adapt recipes for these children. Baby-food recipes are included.

93. Tingey-Michaelis, Carol. *Handicapped Infants and Children*. *See* Chapter 6, item 261.

94. Trimmer, Eric. *Having a Baby: A Complete Guide for the Mother-to-Be*. New York: St. Martin's, 1981.

For expectant parents, this is a practical guide filled with common-sense suggestions and helpful advice. There are sections on heredity, blood groupings, special exercises, diet, pregnancy testing, breast feeding, and things that might go wrong.

95. Varni, James W. *Clinical Behavioral Pediatrics: An Interdisciplinary Biobehavioral Approach*. *See* Chapter 3, item 160.

96. Verrilli, George E., and Anna Marie Mueser. *Welcome Baby: A Guide to the First Six Weeks*. New York: St. Martin's, 1982.

As the title indicates, this is a guide to the baby's first six weeks. The authors suggest their book be used as a checklist of things to take up with one's pediatrician. *Welcome Baby* provides general advice and includes specific information on topics that are important to new mothers. All of the topics are listed in alphabetical order, which this reader finds very helpful. Of interest to some would be the annotated list of books for children also offered.

97. Watkins, Kathleen Pullan. "A Study of the Parent-Child Attachment Bond in Neonatal Intensive Care Nursery Situations: Implications for Program Development." *See* Chapter 3, item 162.

98. Winick, Myron. *Society's Child: Nutrition in Children,*

Diet and Disorders.   Nutley, N.J.: Roche Laboratories, 1980.

Winick views nutrition from a sensible, well-balanced diet approach. In this publication he dispels the many myths of mega-vitamin therapy and points out the potential dangers. Arguments pertaining to possible hazards of salt, sugar, fat and food additives are critically examined. This publication is recommended for its scientific treatment of current issues.

3

SOCIAL-EMOTIONAL DEVELOPMENT IN INFANCY

Kathleen Pullan Watkins

In today's world, the decision to become parents is often
accompanied by tremendous soul searching. Parents-to-be are
eager to provide the very best for their child, considering
their social and economic status as well as willingness to
engage in quality time with a child. One of the primary
reasons for the turn toward such a serious approach to parenting is the suggestion of research that the ties between parents
and their infants influence all other aspects of child development. In fact, it is now known that physical and cognitive
growth during even the earliest months of life may be dependent upon the strength of the parent-child bond.

Experts like Marshall Klaus and John Kennell have suggested that bonding begins even before birth. When parents
share the first fetal movements, select baby names, and plan
their child's future, they are experiencing the first feelings
of love for their unborn infant. After birth, the vast array
of sensory experiences associated with caring for a newborn
act to heighten the protective, nurturing instincts present
in most parents. The appearance, cry, scent, and soft feel
of a neonate become the generators of the bonding process.

It is not until some weeks later, however, that the infant
clearly distinguishes one adult from another. True attachment
is only present when the baby's smile, willingness to be com-
forted, and clinging behaviors are reserved for the few
special adults in the infant's life. As the young child
achieves locomotion, attachment is further demonstrated by
the proximity-seeking behaviors that accompany crawling and
walking.

Psychologist Erik Erikson speaks of this stage in terms
of the child's development of "trust or mistrust." The
securely attached child has an early awareness of his place
and value in the lives of his adults. His curiosity is extensive and is coupled with a strong desire for exploration.
However, this child's interest in the environment is also

tempered by a healthy uncertainty of things and people strange
to him. He will seek out his primary caregivers when the unfamiliar becomes too much, and he expects an environment with
individuals and materials with which he can safely interact.
   What other factors are active in the social-emotional
development of the infant? Soon after the establishment of
the earliest parent-child relations opportunities are present
for the growth of important relationships with other adults,
siblings, and peers. Contrary to what was once believed, the
infant is not merely a passive sensory receptor. After birth
the baby assumes an active role in interactions with others,
indicating needs and feelings through vocalizations, facial
expressions, gestures, and body language. From this point,
the child begins developing "working models" of others. That
is, the young child perceives that the behaviors of others are
fairly predictable. The more frequently a baby interacts with
an individual, the more familiar the child becomes with that
person's regular patterns of behavior, and he learns to respond accordingly. A child who consistently finds emotional
satisfaction in attempts to relate to others learns that interpersonal contact is a pleasurable and rewarding experience.
It is safe to suggest that an infant with many people in his
life who provide attention and loving affection will benefit
from such experience.
   However, to imply that early relationships impact only on
socialization would be to severely underrate their value. It
is through adult-child interactions that much of the infant's
cognitive development originates. Parents and other infant
caregivers provide the stimulus and reinforcement for language
learning, environmental explorations, and early self-awareness.
Without the encouragement provided during play, caregiving
routines, and other family socialization, a child may easily
become the victim of developmental delay with speech, motor,
or cognitive impairment.
   Separation anxiety is an aspect of infant development appearing toward the end of the first year. Although cause for
consternation among parents, seen in the light of its role in
social-emotional development, separation anxiety is a normal
and healthy part of the separation-individuation process.
Incapable of seeing himself as an indivdual, the newborn responds primarily to physical needs and reflexes. By the
eighth month of life, however, the infant has long been responding differentially to familiar and unfamiliar faces and
situations, and his developing feelings direct many of his
behavioral responses to everyday situations. In familiar surroundings, in the company of his primary caregiver, a healthy
infant is likely to appear content and will show that content-
ment by smiling, happy vocalizations, and easy explorations.

Removed from his home and attachment figures, the same infant may behave in a radically different fashion. Quiet crying, withdrawal, or even temper tantrums are among the normal responses of a child experiencing separation anxiety. Although they are not uncommon even in three-year-olds, these symptoms generally disappear with maturity and as a child realizes that he will safely return to home and loved ones.

Among the possible complications to normal social-emotional development is that of emotional loss. Generally resulting from some early trauma, such as the death of or long-term separation from a parent figure or sibling, the impact on infant development can be quite serious. Infants separated from their families under stressful circumstance were first observed by Anna Freud and Dorothy Burlingham during World War II. In studies that have been substantiated by other researchers, these research pioneers found that retarded development, delayed language, chronic mourning, and behavior problems were among the symptoms of the child who has experienced a serious emotional loss. The family that experiences death, separation or family breakup resulting from divorce, a long-distance move, or serious illness is cautioned to remain alert to the emotional needs and behavior of the infant during stressful periods. Many young children are incapable of understanding the emotions experienced and displayed by adults and other children at such times, and the preverbal infant is especially handicapped by the inability to express his own feelings. Parents may not realize that a baby's unusual behavior during a family crisis is probably the result of changes in normal routines and the emotional state of other members of the family. The infant may be blamed for complicating an already upsetting situation by demanding special attention. In reality, the child may be the victim of the stressful circumstances around him.

In addition to those discussed, there are a number of issues of current concern to infant mental health professionals. Four of these merit special attention--parent education, the impact of adolescent pregnancy on the infant, care of the family of the premature or ill baby, and father-child relationships.

At the beginning of this chapter mention was made of the eagerness of many couples to prepare for parenthood. Some of the ways that this goal is accomplished include attendance at preparenting classes and reading a few of the many how-to manuals available on aspects of child rearing. Other parents-to-be consult with pediatricians and psychologists. On the surface, such steps are reasonable preparations for one of life's most important events. Young parents no longer have the large extended families that once provided essential in-

formation and support. However, some child development
specialists are concerned that parents are becoming so fear-
ful of interfering with development, that they are afraid to
make even simple child-rearing decisions without consulting a
specialist. Led to believe that the experts have all the
answers, parents may delay responding to their young children
in situations where a quick response and parental intuition
are of the greatest value.

High among the nationally recognized problems of the
American family are those created by adolescent pregnancy.
The number of births among girls under 18 years of age has
risen steadily in the past decade, prompting research to study
the impact of teenage parenting on the young child. The results of these studies are disconcerting, to say the least.
Frequently lacking in maturity, knowledge of parenting skills,
and support for child rearing, the adolescent mother may be
involved in only minimal interaction with her newborn.

Before her untimely death in 1981, psychologist Selma
Fraiberg studied the disorders frequently associated with
early parenting. Fraiberg expressed concern that young mothers
frequently may recreate in their own lives, with their own
children, the same type of situations through which they were
victimized as children. For the babies of these young women
the results are potentially damaging, unless intense early
intervention can be undertaken. In the most serious cases,
infants observed by Fraiberg suffered from listless and
apathetic behavior, abuse and neglect, nonorganic failure to
thrive, and sleeping and eating disorders. Other researchers
have clearly established the instance of lower intellectual
functioning among the preschool-age children of adolescents,
resulting when parents fail to provide appropriate social
interactions and establish a secure attachment relationship
with their babies. It should be noted, however, that some
teenage parents do receive adequate family support, and even
in instances where this is an absent factor, some manage to
rear children who are emotionally secure and healthy.

Yet another of the infant mental health issues currently
being addressed is that of the emotional care of family and
baby when an infant is premature or ill at birth. Within the
last ten years, as optimal health care has improved the chances
for life for most preterm and sick neonates, attention has
been focused upon other issues relative to the provision of
newborn intensive care. There is more than a suggestion that
early and prolonged separation of parents and infant can have
long-term impact on a baby's physical and emotional well-being
and on family relations. Increased instance of abuse and neglect, nonorganic failure to thrive, behavior problems, and
vulnerable child syndrome (the parents' refusal to accept

their child's wellness after hospital discharge) are among
the potential problems faced when the emotional closeness
essential for healthy bonding and attachment relations fails
to develop. Feelings of guilt, inadequacy, fear for the
child's present and future health condition, and the physical
distance from the newborn required by intensive care have all
been known to interfere with what would normally be a time of
family rejoicing--the birth of a baby. Many newborn special-
care nurseries now assume the role of facilitator of the
parent-infant relationship, providing individual counseling
and support group meetings, finding innovative ways for parents
to participate in infant care, and even following up with home
visiting nursing after the baby's discharge. As yet, the long-
range impact of these efforts is unknown, but many specialists
in infant behavior are hopeful that these and other intervention tools may prove to be effective methods of offsetting
mental health problems in infancy and early childhood.

Last of the issues to be discussed in this chapter is the
role of father-infant relations in child development. For
many years, fathers were considered less important than mothers
in influencing the early social development of their babies.
Relatively recent research has, however, shown that fathers
are equally critical as role models, attachment figures, and
facilitators of overall development. When separate observations were made of mother-child and father-child interactions,
a qualitative difference was found. Mothers observed tended
to be most involved and active with their infants during caregiving routines (diapering and feeding, e.g.), while fathers
were more often initiators of play activities. T. Berry
Brazelton and colleagues even noted variations in body movements depending upon the sex of the parent with whom an infant
was interacting. So fine were the differences noted, that
when videotaping only a baby's arm or leg, trained observers
were able to identify whether the child was with his mother or
father. In all cases, the consensus of the experts is that
fathers should be encouraged to involve themselves in the
lives of their infants to the greatest extent that time and
family situations permit.

Margaret Mahler has suggested that the goal of parent-
child attachment is detachment. The child who receives essential nurturance and develops feelings of self-esteem quickly
begins to see himself as an independent individual capable of
many things. He faces the world eagerly, secure in the knowledge that it holds good things for him. While they may watch
wistfully, his parents do not overprotect or prevent this
growth; instead they are eager to see their child develop into
an autonomous person unafraid of life's challenges.

This chapter has heavily emphasized the role of the
parent in the social-emotional development of the infant.
The reasons for this emphasis are quite simple. Without the
interaction, modeling, and nurturance of parents and primary
caregivers there would be little appropriate emotional development in infancy. Humans are the only species whose infants
are utterly dependent upon the care of adult members for a
prolonged period after birth. So complete is this dependence,
that the provision of food, warmth, and a clean environment
for the baby are, by themselves, inadequate. The fourth essential ingredient, without which an infant can quite literally
die, is love and affection. The parent is both provider and
model of this critical element of development. As teacher of
social skills, a parent by his or her example makes it possible
for the young child to grow into an individual capable of receiving and giving love, understanding and expressing feelings
and needs, and coping successfully in a world that is increasingly demanding and impersonal. Selma Fraiberg wrote,

> ... it appears that parents need not be paragons; they
> may be inexperienced, they may be permitted to err in
> the fashion of the species, and still have an excellent
> chance of rearing a healthy child if the bonds between
> parent and child are strong and provide the incentives
> for growth and development in the child. The decisive
> factors in mental health are the capacities of the ego for
> dealing with conflict, the ability to tolerate frustra-
> tion, to adapt, and to find solutions that bring harmony
> between inner needs and outer reality.

BIBLIOGRAPHY

99.   Ainsworth, Mary D., M.C. Blehar, E. Waters, and S. Wall.
      *Patterns of Attachment: A Psychological Study of the
      Strange Situation.* Hillsdale, N.J.: Erlbaum, 1978.

      Noted attachment specialist Mary Ainsworth and col-
      leagues describe a series of procedures for assessing
      the attachment behavior of infants 11 to 24 months of
      age. Their suggestions from research regarding the impli-
      cations of insecure attachment relationships between in-
      fants and parents also indicate ways of improving the
      quality of infant care at home and in child care settings.

100. Balter, Lawrence. Dr. *Balter's Child Sense: Understand-
     ing and Handling the Common Problems of Infancy and
     Early Childhood.* New York: Poseidon, 1985.

     As "resident child psychologist" for CBS-TV and ABC
     Talkradio, Dr. Balter has helped parents and profession-
     als with his common-sense, comforting approach to child
     rearing. Here in book form is his advice on how to cope
     with the most common behavioral problems of a child's
     first five years.

101. Belsky, Jay, et al. *The Child in the Family.* Reading,
     Mass.: Addison-Wesley, 1984.

     The goal of this important work is to abstract current
     research about the nature of the family and the recipro-
     cal relations between infant and child development and
     parent-child relations. Through a multidisciplinary
     perspective, the authors also address the ways in which
     children affect their parents' behavior and marital rela-
     tions, as well as discussing such family issues as day
     care, divorce, child abuse, and the working couple.

102. Biber, Barbara. *Early Education and Psychological Devel-
     opment.* New Haven, Conn.: Yale University Press, 1984.

     In this important work, the author, an authority in
     early childhood education, presents a selection of her
     essays written during the past four decades.

103. Borman, Kathryn M., ed. *The Social Life of Children in
     a Changing Society.* See Chapter 8, item 347.

104. Bowlby, John. Attachment and Loss Series, Vol. 1.
     Attachment, 2nd ed. New York: Basic Books, 1983.

     This pioneering work is based on years of observation
     by Bowlby and his associates. The text concentrates on
     analyzing the nature of a child's attachment to the
     mother. Empirical data record how young children respond
     to the experience of being separated from, and later
     being reunited with, their mother, with the implications
     of these observations considered as a basis for psycho-
     analytic theory. While later research evidence has con-
     siderably modified this view, the book remains a valuable
     contribution to the literature.

105. Brazelton, T. Berry. *On Becoming a Family: The Growth
     of Attachment.* New York: Delacorte, 1981.

Beginning with the changes brought into the family by pregnancy, the author discusses each step in the bonding process and the emotional process by which parents and babies are eventually bound together into family units. Chapters also focus on the emotional needs of families who have to deal with the special needs created by premature and Caesarian births.

106. Bronfenbrenner, Urie. *The Ecology of Human Development: Experiments by Nature and Design.* Cambridge, Mass.: Harvard University Press, 1979.

Dr. Bronfenbrenner, one of the great minds of our time, has offered a new theoretical perspective for research in human development filled with exciting and challenging possibilities. As defined by Bronfenbrenner in more abstract terms, the ecological environment is "conceived as extending far beyond the immediate situation directly effecting the developing person--the objects to which he responds or the people with whom he interacts on a face-to-face basis.... Contrasting with prevailing research models ... the principle of interconnectedness is seen as applying not only within settings, but with equal force and consequence to linkages between settings...."

107. Close, Sylvia. *The Toddler and the New Baby.* Boston: Routledge & Kegan Paul, 1980.

Close offers step-by-step guidelines to expectant parents with a toddler already part of the family. She deals with typical examples of problems that may arise and shows how such problems can be either prevented or overcome.

108. Coffin, Patricia. *1, 2, 3, 4, 5, 6: How to Understand and Enjoy the Years That Count.* New York: Collier Books, 1972.

The author, a mother and a journalist, recorded the first six years of her daughter's life with a blend of sensitive photographs and relevant text. This is a personal as well as professional account of a child's development and should be helpful to other parents in their understanding their own child's early years.

109. Cohen, Jean-Pierre. *Childhood: The First Six Years.* *See* Chapter 2, item 40.

110. Comer, James P., and Alvin F. Poussaint. *Black Child Care: How to Bring Up a Healthy Black Child in America.* New York: Pocket Books, 1975.

     Comer and Poussaint's guide for parents rearing black children deals with questions of racial identity, prejudice, and general child-rearing problems.

111. Divas, Mirille. *I'm a Year Old Now.* Englewood Cliffs, N.J.: Prentice-Hall, 1983.

     This volume is translated from the French book *J'ai l'an.* The author, a French clinical psychologist who specializes in infancy, has written a unique child-rearing book that sees the picture from the infant's point of view . The text is a charming as well as informative treatment of the myriad everyday situations that arise in the first 24 months of life.

112. Dunn, Judy. *Distress and Comfort.* Cambridge: Harvard University Press, 1977.

     Dunn considers some of the work on causes of distress during childhood. She explores the various reactions of children to both stress and comforting and studies a variety of evidence relating to everything from the first cry to complex social interactions. In addition, she reviews most of the relevant theories.

113. Durrell, Doris. *The Critical Years: A Guide for Dedicated Parents.* Oakland, Calif.: New Harbinger, 1984.

     Here is a book for parents who like to have theoretical terminology translated into jargon-free language. Chapters discuss the difficult baby, the easy baby, sleep behavior, group day care, temper tantrums, tears, and the like.

114. Fraiberg, Selma. *Clinical Studies in Infant Mental Health: The First Year of Life.* New York: Basic Books, 1980.

     In the introduction the author states that in the past 20 years "clinical and developmental research in infancy [has] given us answers to a multitude of questions that once seemed unanswerable." This book provides a body of knowledge gathered by Fraiberg and her colleagues, including their methods for arriving at clinical assessments and outlines for treatment designed to bring about measurable and positive change.

115. Fraiberg, Selma. *Every Child's Birthright: In Defense of Mothering*. New York: Basic Books, 1977.

     The question is raised of what it is all infants need and what they have a given right to expect in the way of care and love. The author, as in her classic *The Magic Years*, shows parents and professionals how to bridge the gap between "what is known," and stored in the library and "what is practiced" in the rearing of infants."

116. Fraiberg, Selma. *The Magic Years: Understanding and Handling the Problems of Early Childhood*. New York: Scribner, 1959.

     Written with warmth and sensitivity, *The Magic Years* is a classic in the field of emotional development of children from birth through preschool age.

117. Freud, Anna, and D. Burlingham. *Infants Without Families*. New York: International University Press, 1944.

     This volume contains one of the earliest studies of the impact on young children of separation from their parents. Conducted in World War II England's Hampstead Nurseries, this research project included an experiment with "artifical families" and contains results of attachment and loss studies that are supported by current research.

118. Gelfand, Donna M., and Donald P. Hartmann. *Child Behavior Analysis and Therapy*. New York: Pergamon, 1984.

     Like its predecessor, the expanded and revised second edition is designed to help students understand how to begin and complete behavioral modification studies with infants and children. Primarily meant to be used as a text in classes and to serve as an aid under supervised instruction, the comprehensive clear-cut presentation makes it a valuable addition to the literature.

119. Greenspan, Stanley I. *Psychopathology and Adaption in Infancy and Early Childhood: Principles of Clinical Diagnosis and Preventive Intervention*. New York: International Universities Press, 1981.

     This monograph, based on the author's approach to structural theory of development, is the first in a series planned by the National Center for Clinical Infant Programs. Although a complex subject, the text is written in clear and understandable terms, making this book valuable not only to professionals, but to parents as well.

120. Greenspan, Stanley I., and Nancy Thorndike Greenspan. *First Feelings: Milestones in the Emotional Development of Your Baby and Child.* New York: Viking, 1985.

     Using a six-stage framework, the authors describe the progress of emotional development. *First Feelings* describes Greenspan's own theories of infant development.

121. Jackson, Jane Flannery, and Joseph H. Jackson. *Infant Culture.* New York: Crowell, 1978.

     The authors explore the research literature on infants and describe many key findings provided by developmental psychologists. The focus is in the area of social development and communication. The volume should be of interest to professionals and parents.

122. Kagan, Jerome. *The Nature of the Child.* New York: Basic Books, 1984.

     Controversial and challenging, Kagan's unique interpretation of human development makes fascinating reading. Contrary to conventional view, Kagan argues, perhaps persuasively, that early experience does not rigidly shape our lives but that as humans we have a life-long ability for change. Beautifully written, as all of Kagan's work, this evocative book is one that scholars and parents will want to read.

123. Kagan, Jerome, Richard B. Kearsley, and Philip R. Zelazo. *Infancy: Its Place in Human Development.* Cambridge: Harvard University Press, 1980.

     The basic stimulus for writing this book was to share the results of research that was concerned with the effects of group care on the child's psychological development. While raising important questions, this work provides thought-provoking data that seems to demonstrate that day care at its best may not be detrimental. Although this issue is still far from resolved, the findings are encouraging and hopeful.

124. Klaus, Marshall H., and John H. Kennell. *Parent-Infant Bonding,* 2nd ed. St. Louis: Mosby, 1982.

     The authors attempt to tie in research on animal and human behavior to support and promote the concept of parent-infant bonding. They describe the steps in this relationship as established before and immediately after birth and suggest the need for hospitals to aid rather than hinder this important emotional tie. A separate chapter addresses the bonding and grief processes presented by prematurity, neonatal illness and death, congenital malformation, and stillbirth.

125. Lamb, Michael E., ed. *The Role of the Father in Child Development*, 2nd ed. New York: Wiley, 1981.

This series of articles describes the impact of fathering on infant and young child development. Father's impact on socialization, sex role identification, moral internalization, and cognitive growth are discussed, as are fathers' roles in other cultures and father's absence from family life.

126. Lask, Bryan. *Overcoming Behavior Problems in Children*. New York: Arco, 1985.

All of the common problems of behavior in young children are discussed and put into perspective with sound and sympathetic advice.

127. Leach, Penelope. *Babyhood*, 2nd ed. *See* Chapter 1, item 15.

128. Leavenworth, Carol, et al. *Family Living*. *See* Chapter 7, item 308.

129. Leboyer, Frederick. *Loving Hands*. New York: Knopf, 1976.

Leboyer shows how to use the traditional art of baby massage in order to communicate love and strength to a newborn. Beautiful photographs complement the poetic text.

130. Lewis, Michael, and Leonard A. Rosenblum, eds. *The Effect of the Infant on Its Caregiver*. New York: Wiley, 1974.

Volume I of the series The Origins of Behavior centers on the significance of the interaction between caregiver and infant and the subtle, yet strong, influence each has on the other in shaping their ongoing dyadic behavior. This volume is the result of a conference sponsored by the Educational Testing Service, Princeton, N.J., and represents a variety of viewpoints and data drawn from many levels of discourse.

131. Lickona, Thomas. *Raising Good Children*. New York: Bantam, 1983.

Lickona contends that just as parents learn how to foster their children's physical, intellectual, emotional, and social development, they can nurture moral development. The author describes six stages of moral development plus guidelines for raising children to become decent, caring, and responsible members of society. Of special interest is the chapter on "Babies: The Beginnings of Moral Development."

132. Lief, Nina R., with Mary Ellen Fahs, ed. *The First Year of Life: A Guide for Parents*. New York: Dodd, Mead, 1982.

The authors feel that while much research has been done on the importance of a child's earliest years, little of this information reaches parents. Their book links developmental theory with appropriate application, thus enabling parents and caregivers to see how childrearing methods directly influence an infant's total development. Such topics are covered as parents' feelings about the child; sleeping, waking, feeding; toilet training; discipline vs. punishment; etc.

133. Mac, Roddy. *Child Rearing: What to Do Now!* West Allis, Wisc.: Pine Mountain, 1984.

The strength of this book is its spectrum of childrearing suggestions for parents that allow for choice and the adherence to personal values.

134. *Infants: The New Knowledge*. *See* Chapter 4, item 183.

135. McClinton, Barbara S., and Blanche G. Meier. *Beginnings: Psychology of Early Childhood*. St. Louis: Mosby, 1978.

This is a text designed for introductory child development courses, providing the student in applied training programs with a solid background of psychological principles. Included are materials on the infant, the preschooler, and the young child in the first year of school. Writing in an informal style, the authors have maintained a balance between theory and research as well as practical application.

136. Mahler, Margaret S., Fred Pine, and Anni Bergman. *The Psychological Birth of the Human Infant: Symbiosis and Individuation*. New York: Basic Books, 1975.

A landmark in the psychoanalytic literature, this work represents an important breakthrough toward the understanding of infant development. Separation and individuation are seen as two complementary developments--intertwined, but not identical. Although much is technical, it is a well-written, readable book and can be recommended for parents as well as professionals.

137. Maxim, George W. *The Very Young: Guiding Children from Infancy Through the Early Years*. *See* Chapter 4, item 189.

138. Moore, Shirley G., and Catherine R. Cooper, eds. *The Young Child*. Reviews of Research, Vol. 3. Washington, D.C.: National Association for the Education of Young Children, 1982.

The authors provide an introductory chapter on the application of research by practitioners and then review research findings in child development. The topics selected focus on socioemotional beginnings, language and thinking, social relationships, physical development, and special needs. Unlike volumes 1 and 2 of this series, the text has been written expressly for this volume. Students, as well as practicing professionals, will find the volume interesting.

139. Oppenheim, Joanne, et al. *Raising a Confident Child: The Bank Street Year-by-Year Guide*. New York: Pantheon, 1984.

Balancing between the matter-of-fact aspects of child development and child rearing and the more subtle, complex features that surround each stage of growth, this book combines philosophical guidelines with concrete, step-by-step suggestions. For parents and educators alike, this should be a helpful volume.

140. Pelligrini, Anthony, and Thomas D. Yawkey. *The Development of Oral and Written Language in Social Contexts*. *See* Chapter 5, item 230.

141. Provence, Sally A., and Rose C. Lipton. *Infants in Institutions: A Comparison of Their Development with Family-Reared Infants During the First Year of Life*. New York: International Universities Press, 1978.

This report is written primarily for professionals in the field of infant care. Based on a research study of

institutionalized infants as compared with infants
raised in a family setting, the authors, both prominent
physicians, see group care inadquate in meeting infants'
needs. While not an indictment against any institution
and staff, a plea is made for greater understanding of
the complex process of development as a foundation for
better care for babies.

142. Ribble, Margaret A. *The Rights of Infants: Early Psychological Needs and Their Satisfaction*, 2nd ed. *See*
Chapter 7, item 324.

143. Richards, M. *Infancy: World of the Newborn*. New York:
Harper & Row, 1979.

Richards, a psychologist, in his authoritative presentation dispels the helplessness that afflicts many
parents caring for a newborn child. In his comprehensive
volume he considers infant development, parental responses,
practical baby care, and infant development. He covers
growth and feeding, sleeping and crying, newborn capabilities, learning how to move and think, communication
and games, the end of infancy, and relationships between
boys and girls and fathers and mothers.

144. Roiphe, Herman, and Eleanor Galenson. *Infantile Origins
of Sexual Identity*. New York: International Universities Press, 1981.

Basing their findings on a study of more than 70 infants, the authors report compelling evidence that
points to a definite genital awareness and beginning
sense of gender identity in very young children. This
is an important book in the area of psychoanalytic research study of infant behavior that should be helpful
to professionals in the field of infant development.

145. Rothenberg, Mira. *Children with Emerald Eyes: Histories
of Extraordinary Boys and Girls*. New York: Dial, 1977.

Rothenberg provides the reader with a startling,
sensitive, and informative account of a teacher's work
with autistic children.

146. Rubin, Kenneth H., and Hildy S. Ross. *Peer Relationships
and Social Skills in Childhood*. *See* Chapter 8, item
379.

147. Salk, Lee. *The Complete Dr. Salk: An A-to-Z Guide to
Raising Your Child*. New York: World Almanac, 1983.

In his many years as a practicing psychologist, the author has gained much insight into the various factors that contribute to emotional disorders in children. While emotional illness can be treated in later years, it is much easier to prevent problems from arising by avoiding the causes in infancy and early childhood. This book is written to help parents avoid emotional disturbance and foster the child's fullest potential through the understanding of the child's developmental process. Alphabetically arranged, this excellent guide touches on topics such as anger, baby talk, fears, head banging, intelligence quotient, left-handedness, naps, only child, pacifier, sleep, and toilet training.

148. Salk, Lee. *Your Child's First Year*. New York: Cornerstone, 1983.

Believing that a good first year is the basis for a lifetime of emotional and physical well-being, Salk offers information and suggestions for making your baby's first year a happy and secure one. Chapter 1 deals with the issue of choosing to be a parent. The next three chapters discuss life with the newborn, choosing to breast feed or bottle feed, and the baby's emotional needs. Discipline and advice for coping with your own needs is explored. The final chapters deal with special problems and coping with sibling rivalry.

149. Schaffer, Rudolph. *Mothering*. Cambridge: Harvard University Press, 1977.

Part of The Developing Child Series, this volume presents a review of traditional theories on child rearing and goes on to research that reflects on the unprecedented advances in recent research on human development and the relationship between mother and child.

150. Segal, Julius, and Zelda Segal. *Growing Up Smart and Happy*. New York: McGraw-Hill, 1985.

Here the authors strive to answer fully parents' questions about the intellectual and psychological development of children. They place the current focus on "superkids" into perspective and emphasize allowing children to experience the milestones in their development at a natural pace. Although written for parents and caregivers, the material presented should be helpful to educators and health professionals as well.

151. Sherrod, Kathryn, and Peter Vietze. *Infancy.* Monterey, Calif.: Brooks/Cole, 1978.

    The authors treat the study of human infant develop-ment in the context of the social environment in which infants live. At the same time they take an empirical view that presents information relating to well-estab-lished recent research. Parents and students in family life, early childhood education, human development, health fields, and psychology will find useful informa-tion.

152. Singer, Dorothy, and Jerome Singer. *Partner in Play: A Step-by-Step Guide to Imaginative Play in Children.* See Chapter 8, item 384.

153. Smart, Mollie S., and Russell C. Smart. *Infants: Devel-opment and Relationships,* 2nd ed. New York: Macmillan, 1978.

    This book, primarily a text for students, is concerned with the early interaction between infant and adult and the impact this relationship has on the child's physi-cal, mental, and emotional development. Each of the five chapters consists of a text section followed by readings that report research or review topics concern-ing infants. Included is a short but informative course in statistics.

154. Sroufe, Alan. *Knowing and Enjoying Your Baby.* Englewood Cliffs, N.J.: Prentice-Hall, 1977.

    The focus here is on the child's emotional development. Sroufe has written a practical guide that shows parents how they can be a positive influence on their child's emotional health and why the infant-caregiver relation-ship is vital, with far-reaching implications for the future.

155. Stone, Jeanette Galambos. *A Guide to Discipline,* rev. ed. Washington, D.C.: National Association for the Education of Young Children, 1978.

    Stone suggests many techniques for promoting positive behavior and cooperation in young children. Parents and educators will better understand the role of development in youngsters' ability to behave appropriately.

156. Stone, L. Joseph, and Joseph Church. *Childhood and Adolescence: A Psychology of the Growing Person,* 5th ed. New York: Random House, 1984.

The latest edition of this classic text continues to
deal in great detail with the early years. Five chapters are devoted to infancy--prenatal environmental
influences, prenatal development and birth, the newborn
baby (including father-infant relations), attachment,
and practical issues in infant care. There is a chapter
on the latest findings on infant's cognitive abilities
and early influences on development and the reversibility
and prevention of adverse rearing conditions. The topic
of toddlerhood (with new emphasis on early social cognition) is expanded with a chapter on language development
and its central role in behavior and total development.
As in previous editions, the book makes its points
clearly, matching up-to-the-minute research findings
with guidelines for practical application.

157. Stone, L. Joseph, Henrietta T. Smith, and Lois B. Mur-
      phy, eds. *The Competent Infant: Research and Commen-
      tary*. See Chapter 4, item 204.

158. Stoutt, Glenn R., Jr. *The First Month of Life: A Parent's
      Guide to the Care of the Newborn*. See Chapter 2, item
      91.

159. Tronick, Edward, and Lauren Adamson. *Babies as People:
      New Findings on Our Social Beginnings*. New York: Mac-
      millan, 1980.

      Basing their conclusions on recent research in infant
      development, the authors show clearly and sensitively
      that babies, far from being helpless, come into this
      world able to perceive and act and eager to learn about
      and interact with their new environment and the people
      in their lives. Valuable insights are given that will
      guide parents in learning how to listen to the newborn's
      communication and how to respond most effectively.

160. Varni, James W. *Clinical Behavioral Pediatrics: An
      Interdisciplinary Biobehavioral Approach*. New York:
      Pergamon, 1983.

      An emerging approach to care of children with physical
      handicaps and chronic diseases, termed "Behavioral
      Pediatrics," represents an interdisciplinary and com-
      prehensive field of study that is receiving clinical
      attention as well as application. This text provides
      an overview of this technique for the advanced student
      and clinician in pediatric medicine.

161. Walters, C. Etta, ed. *Mother-Infant Interaction.* New
     York: Human Sciences Press, 1976.

     Here the focus is on mother-infant interaction in the
     emotional, social, and cognitive areas of the infant's
     development. The chapters are written by a number of
     specialists, and the materials presented are based on
     research studies and neurologic and psychoanalytic
     findings. Useful as a basic undergraduate text for
     courses in child development, this book might be of in-
     terest to parents as well.

162. Watkins, Kathleen Pullan. "A Study of the Parent-Child
     Attachment Bond in Neonatal Intensive Care Nursery
     Situations: Implications for Program Development."
     Unpublished doctoral dissertation. Philadelphia:
     Temple University, 1983.

     This study includes a review of the history and theory
     of attachment behavior. Factors known to interfere
     with the bonding and attachment processes are discussed,
     with special attention to those situations presented by
     prematurity or illness at birth. Suggestions are pro-
     vided for the development of parent-infant emotional
     support programs to meet the needs of these families.

163. Weininger, Otto. *Play and Education: The Basic Tool to
     Early Childhood Learning. See* Chapter 8, item 390.

164. Weissbourd, Bernice, and Judith S. Musick, eds. *In-
     fants: Their Social Environments.* Washington, D.C.:
     National Association for the Education of Young
     Children, 1981.

     The authors address the many critical issues surround-
     ing the caregiving settings of the first three years in
     a child's life. Research is examined and guidelines
     given for designing and implementing appropriate infant
     and toddler environments. The book is directed at edu-
     cators, health care professionals, and social policy
     makers.

165. Wilson, Amos N. *The Developmental Psychology of the
     Black Child.* New York: Africana Research Publica-
     tions, 1978.

     This book presents an in-depth description of the world
     of the black child and at the same time examines parent-
     hood from a black perspective. The author states that
     psychology and the social sciences, as they are presently

constituted, do not meet the needs of black children. Guidelines are given to professionals in these fields to help meet the special challenges. While aimed at the professional, it should also be valuable to black parents and all concerned with the special problems of the black family.

166. Wyckoff, Jerry, and Barbara C. Unell. *Discipline Without Shouting or Spanking*. New York: Meadowbrook, 1984.

The authors have subtitled their book "Practical Solutions to the Most Common Preschool Behavior Problems," and in fact every effort is made to give suggestions on how to deal with and how to prevent behavior problems. Although it would seem that discipline has no place in the child rearing of an infant, it is surprising how often new parents are concerned with "spoiling" even the youngest baby. From bedtime problems to resisting car seats, the guidelines given are easy to follow and well tested.

COGNITIVE DEVELOPMENT IN INFANCY

Kathleen Pullan Watkins

In the seventeenth century, philosopher John Locke called the newborn "tabula rasa," that is, in a blank state at birth, devoid of any prior learning or immediate capabilities. Ideas about the passivity of babies remained constant until relatively recent times, when, at long last, researchers began to make headway in charting the unexplored reaches of the human brain. We now know that the infant's learning begins in utero and a variety of competencies are present even at the moment of birth. Far from being passive, the newborn is equipped and ready for learning.

Within 3 weeks of conception, the embryotic brain begins developing. The most rapid growth occurs between 8 and 13 weeks of gestational age. At birth, those portions of the brain that control essential functions, such as respiration and circulation, are fully operational. Other parts, controlling mobility and speech, mature more slowly.

Although weighing just one pound at birth, the brain gains a second pound in the first 12 months of extrauterine life. The majority of this growth occurs in the lower rear portion of the brain, or cerebellum, which controls fine and gross motor coordination. It takes more than a decade for the third pound of brain matter to develop, but the result is a logically thinking, communicative, and independent youngster.

The development of neurons, the primary units of the brain, is also completed during the first year. It is the networking of neurons that makes thinking, performing complex tasks, and even going about daily routines occur smoothly through the integration of conscious and unconscious brain activity. Like other aspects of brain growth, neural expansion occurs in spurts, and each time unfolding cognitive abilities are produced.

Research specialists have added much to our new knowledge of the brain. Among the foremost of these is Paul MacLean of

the National Institute of Mental Health, who developed the
theory of the "triune brain." MacLean suggests that there
are three primary layers of brain matter that function together to perform tasks from the simplest to the most complex.
These layers are the reptilian complex, the limbic system,
and the neocortex. The innermost of these areas, the reptilian complex, is located at the end of the brain stem.
First to develop, it controls the most primitive and basic
of human functions and drives.

The secondary layer, the limbic system, regulates moods,
emotions, and social behavior. The limbic system produces
powerful chemicals called "endorphins," which influence such
things as an individual's emotional state on any given day or
response to physical extremes like pain or fatigue.

The outermost area of the brain, the neocortex, regulates
speech, writing abilities, problem solving, and other intri-
cate forms of cognitive functioning. The two hemispheres of
the neocortex, left and right, serve different purposes. The
left acts as the processor of abstract and rational thought,
and the right regulates the sensory information that enables
an individual to see the whole of something rather than always focusing only on its parts. It is in the right hemisphere
of the brain that human creativity is generated.

At present, there are two main schools of thought regarding the way in which learning takes place, the developmental
and the behaviorist. Although the former is favored by most
early childhood educators, behaviorists are, nonetheless, extremely influential in the arena of the ever developing framework of schooling for children of all ages.

Among the recognized experts in the field of learning
theory is B.F. Skinner, a modern spokesperson who has made
numerous contributions to the continuing study of the learning
process. Skinner calls his theory "operant conditioning," and
he emphasizes reinforcement as the most important aspect of
what and how an individual learns. Any behavior emitted by
an organism Skinner calls "operant." The frequency with
which operants reoccur is largely dependent upon the reinforcement the organism receives or that which immediately follows
the behavior.

For example, within the first few months of life many
infants become aware that their crying elicits a particular
response from their parents. For some, that response is
cuddling or soothing words, but for others the response received is anger. The baby's response (behavior) is soon altered by the type of reinforcement given by mother and father.
Reinforcement can also work to the disadvantage of parent and
child. A youngster who consistently receives desirable rewards
for negative behavior may, by age two or three, become quite

manipulative. Observe the two-year-old who is given a coveted toy after throwing a temper tantrum. While the toy may temporarily soothe the child's anger, it also provides strong motivation for the toddler to repeat the tantrum the next time the parent says, "No." By contrast, when positive reinforcement follows only those behaviors considered desirable by parental standards, the child learns to perform cooperatively.

There is some evidence that operant conditioning may be successful in work with children with mental retardation and those with learning, or behavior problems. However, many experts with opposing views question the wisdom of the regular use of this approach. Opponents believe that operant conditioning can result in a child's dependency on external motivation in order to learn.

The cognitive developmentalist approach is based upon the theories of Jean Piaget. Piaget combined biologic and epistemologic knowledge in propositions which suggest that human biological structure combined with environment and manipulation of things in it are the producers of intelligence. The most obvious difference between this and the behaviorist viewpoint is that according to developmentalists, children have some degree of control over their own learning. Piaget stated that all individuals seek to reach a state of intellectual balance, or equilibrium, between what is known and what is being processed and will be learned.

A clear illustration of this process was regularly provided in the lectures of the late Dr. Lois Macomber of Temple University, who was one of the foremost experts in Piagetian theory. Macomber used the example of the infant, who at approximately 15 months of age is exposed to an unfamiliar animal. At first, the child seeks to relate this animal to a known pet by pointing and saying, "Doggie." Piaget called this process "assimilation." When parents point out the differences, this creature is much larger, has very big ears, and a long nose, and name this new animal "elephant," the child "accommodates" this information by creating both a new category and by enlarging the concept of things called "animals." The result is what Piaget termed "equilibrium."

Piaget suggested that cognitive development occurs in four stages—the sensory motor, preoperational, concrete, and formal operations stages. The first, or sensory motor stage, lasts approximately two years. In the beginning of this phase, neonatal behaviors are primarily reflexive. Startling, sucking, and grasping are examples of these. Soon, however, through the dual processes of assimilation and accommodation, new behaviors become evident. One of those most characteristic of the sensory motor stage is object permanence. This is

the name given to the skill of recognizing that an object
still exists even when removed from sight, as when an adult
hides a toy under a blanket.

Accompanying early motor development is another characteristic of the sensory motor stage called "causality." An
infant learns about the cause-effect relationship as a sense
of control over the environment develops. When a baby pushes
away a bowl or spoon, it may fall clattering to the floor
spilling food all about. As the child discovers that this
messy effect is the result of pushing the bowl, such per-
formances may become a daily routine accompanied by giggles
of delight. Many parents are unaware that the infant has an
egocentric nature and is unable to recognize the mess created
or understand the dismay of mother and daddy. However, as a
growing number of parents are educated about aspects of child
development, many are able to sit back and enjoy all the
triumphs of infancy.

Cognitive skills learned in early childhood, including
classifying, comparison and contrast, and recognizing patterns,
are some of the abilities that enable a child to sort and use
information accurately. When classifying, a youngster mentally arranges information according to some established cri-
teria. People, animals, and food items, for example, are
things that are recognized quite early as having distinctly
different characteristics. Comparison and contrast skills
require the child to perceive likenesses and differences in
objects while studying simple attributes, such as color,
texture, and shape. Seeing patterns is the process of recognizing similarities in design or arrangement. One of the
first patterns understood by babies is that presented by the
human face. Even neonates respond differentially to pictures
of eyes, nose, and mouth presented in the appropriate configu-
ration. With the growth of language in the second year,
rhyming words become yet another type of recognizable pattern.

During infancy, parents and other primary caregivers must
be observant to signs of cognitive growth, much as to the in-
dications of other aspects of development. There are specific
behavioral indicators of age-appropriate cognitive functioning
just as for physical and social-emotional learning.

Even before six months of age, an infant should evidence
a number of discriminatory abilities. Newborns are able to
follow objects with their eyes for short distances and will
respond differentially to a variety of noises, ranging from
sharp sounds, like clapping hands, to a parent's voice. At
first, visual following is only horizontal, but it soon becomes vertical as well. As babies become able to hold their
heads erect, they begin scanning and studying the surrounding
environment in all directions.

By the middle of the first year, an infant is capable of more refined forms of discrimination, such as recognizing feeding apparatus and responding to familiar shapes and faces. Other forms of differentiation apparent at this time include the infant's beginning ability to respond to certain receptive vocabulary. Terms of greeting (bye-bye), object words (cookie), and the baby's own name are examples of these. As the months pass, object permanence appears, and the child becomes able to search for and locate hidden or disappearing objects. At this point, older infants will also show surprise when confronted by discrepancies or deviations from what they accept as usual.

Performance of these competencies is entirely dependent upon the development of the sort of cognitive skills previously described. While at the outset the infant's skills are simple, maturation and experience soon produce more complicated behaviors.

In ever growing numbers, people are interested in how cognitive development takes place and which factors act to enhance it. Despite current disagreement about the appropriateness of pushing infants into academic learning situations, there is general concurrence that early sensory, motor, and language experiences with supportive adults can be beneficial to even the youngest child.

For some time researchers have been certain that there are factors in infancy that can inhibit or enhance brain growth and later intellectual performance. Malnutrition, lack of sensory stimulation, and even the absence of parental affection may have long-term effects on cognitive development. On the other hand, early intellectual stimulation, a nurturing environment, and sound nutrition may positively influence brain growth.

Infant development or "stimulation" programs are a formalized method of promoting the development of the whole child, aimed at helping babies get a head start in reaching individual potential. First designed for children designated at-risk or with specific developmental delay, these programs are now catering to the normal child whose parents are concerned about maximizing growth in the precious years of early childhood. Without speculating as to an infant's long-range capabilities, and at the same time ever mindful of the signs of developmental problems, such programs offer an environment devoted to sensory exploration, manipulation, and discovery.

Infant "educarers," as specialist Magda Gerber calls them, have learned that one does not "teach" babies, but rather leads them to learning. By providing a safe and healthy environment equipped with age-appropriate materials, and by talking to and playing with infants, they learn at a rate that meets their own, rather than adult, needs.

Infant stimulation programs place no limits on children's abilities. Each baby is observed, worked with, and responded to as an individual with limitless capabilities. Interactions, materials, and experiences are directed toward cognitive, language, self-help, motor, and social development. Research shows that an infant's intellectual growth does not occur in isolation but is heavily dependent upon corresponding growth in other areas.

When an infant plays peek-a-boo with a caregiver, for example, a number of types of learning occur. As a game, peek-a-boo is a social activity that provides instruction in simple rules of play, enhances the adult-child relationship, and produces pleasure for the participants. The game's hand movements are an exercise for developing fine muscles. Through the hide-and-seek nature of the play, the baby also takes steps toward the growth of object permanence, an important aspect of the sensory motor stage, according to Piaget.

Infant stimulation programs tend to provide many experiences of this type in a milieu purposefully designed to promote children's natural curiosity. Bright primary colors are often used, and materials are simply arranged at babies' eye and reach levels. Toys are selected to make a variety of sensory experiences possible, and even before the onset of locomotion, infants are often placed on soft, warm floor surfaces, inviting them to explore from the first months of life. The key to effective learning experiences in infancy, however, is most definitely to be found in the quality of caregiving. Adults must be willing stimulators of infant interest in surrounding people and things, must be quick to respond to interests once they are demonstrated, and must frequently and genuinely praise each achievement made in infancy.

In his outstanding volume, *The First Three Years of Life*, Burton White suggests that good parenting and caregiving can be achieved without extraordinary measures. Regular caretaking routines are also learning experiences. Feeding, bathing, changing, car and carriage rides provide valuable opportunities for sensory stimulation and the storage of information in a growing body of knowledge. Many ordinary household items are entirely appropriate as infant toys, White states, putting to rest the idea that educating an infant can only be achieved through the use of expensive commercially made products.

It may be wise to remember that the remarkable Maria Montessori suggested that there are special periods for all sorts of learning, phases that cannot be engineered by adults, only recognized and supported. Infancy is, indeed, a special time. Important physiological growth takes place that is the precursor and enabler of a lifetime of learning. This development must be gently coaxed by caring adults who understand the fragile nature of a desire for and love of learning. To smother this interest in infancy with reading and math lessons, or flash card exercises designed for older learners, may be to impose a devastating handicap. Cognitive development can and will occur with time, loving nurturance, and opportunities to explore and know the surrounding world.

BIBLIOGRAPHY

167. Adler, Sol, et al., eds. *Lesson Plans for the Infant and Toddler: A Sequential Oral Communications Program for Clinicians and Teachers.* Springfield, Ill.: Thomas, 1984.

The lesson plans outlined are designed to provide infants and toddlers with intensive multisensory stimulation within a warm and responsive environment. Although speech-language clinicians will find this book most useful, it should be helpful also to parents and preschool educators--Head Start, kindergarten, nursery, and daycare personnel.

168. Bailey, Rebecca Anne, and Elsie Carter Burton. *The Dynamic Self: Activities to Enhance Infant Development.* St. Louis: Mosby, 1982.

The title reflects both the volume's theme and purpose. Stress is placed on the key role the infant years have in the development of a child's fundamental learning skills. Guidelines are provided that mesh theory with practical application of the activities, which can be easily adapted by teachers as well as professionals.

169. Berg, Leila. *Reading and Loving.* See Chapter 10, item 454.

170. Bower, T.G.R. *Development in Infancy.* San Francisco: Freeman, 1974.

Calling into question both the extreme nativist position as well as the extreme empiricist position, the author considers methods currently used for the study of infants, as well as some of the results. Focus is on

the importance of the psychological environment of the
developing infant in accelerating or impeding the at-
tainment of cognitive skills.

171. Brunner, Jerome. *Human Growth and Development.* New
York: Oxford University Press, 1978.

Presented are a series of lectures by leading scholars
in the fields of psychology, psychiatry, and education
that offer insights into some of the biological, social,
and political factors involved in growing up in our
complex society. Included are guidelines for the practical application of some of the findings explored.

172. Cass-Beggs, Barbara. *Your Baby Needs Music.* New York:
St. Martin's, 1978.

For parents and teachers who think they are not musical, and even those who think they are, this is a helpful book. For the child from birth to age two, there
are five sections for each stage of development: croons,
which is half-speaking rather than singing, lullabies,
finger rhymes, action songs, and playing musical instru-
ments.

173. Castle, Kathryn. *The Infant and Toddler Handbook: Invitations for Optimum Early Development.* Atlanta:
Humanics, 1983.

Extending "invitations" to infants and toddlers means
providing learning invitations to look, listen, touch,
and communicate—learning activities that foster all
areas of development: physical, emotional, cognitive,
and social. Translating child development research
into suggestions for practical application, the author
has organized the activities into a ready-to-use infant
curriculum for home or group care. Additionally, she
discusses concerns about safety, arranging indoor space,
basic care routines, bedtime, and toy selection.

174. Coffin, Patricia. *1, 2, 3, 4, 5, 6: How to Understand
and Enjoy the Years That Count.* See Chapter 3, item
108.

175. Gordon, Ira J. *The Infant Experience.* Columbus, Ohio:
Merrill, 1975.

A classic, this book is designed for the practitioner
and reflects the belief in the "importance of the parent
as teacher, the infant as a competent learner." Written

in clear, readable language, it combines theory with practical application and should be helpful to parents and professionals. The late Dr. Gordon was most concerned about increasing the number of parents who understand their infant and are ready to make the infant experience what it should be--"a great beginning for the child's exploration of self and world."

176. Haith, Marshall M. *Rules That Babies Look By: The Organization of Newborn Visual Activity.* Hillsdale, N.J.: Erlbaum, 1980.

Recent innovative methodologies and technologies have given new insight to the understanding of early infancy. Haith limits himself to a discussion of the infant's visual world. Written principally with the student of psychology and the academic researcher in mind, the book can also benefit other professionals interested in early behavior.

177. Honig, Alice S. *Playtime Learning Games for Young Children.* Syracuse, N.Y.: Syracuse University Press, 1982.

This practical and imaginative book provides simple-to-follow instructions for games designed to teach thinking skills to children from age two through kindergarten. The author, an internationally recognized consultant on child development, has designed 24 games that require little time on the part of the parent or caregiver, while at the same time providing a rich learning experience for the child.

178. Johnson, Robert Leland. *Super Babies: A Handbook of Enriched and Accelerated Childhood Development.* Smithtown, N.Y.: Exposition Press, 1982.

The volume is basically a progress report, written by a father whose child took part in an experimental (and highly controversial program at Glenn Doman's Institutes for the Achievement of Human Potential. Included is a bibliography, a list of vitamin sources, addresses of suppliers of educational materials, and a checklist of some of the characteristics of gifted and talented children that parents can use for screening their own child's possible giftedness.

179. Johnson & Johnson Baby Products Company. *The First Wondrous Year: You and Your Baby.* See Chapter 7, item 300.

180. Leahey, Thomas H., and Richard J. Harris. *Human Learning.* Englewood Cliffs, N.J.: Prentice-Hall, 1985.

Although human learning and how individuals change and adapt to changing circumstances is the main focus, the authors do consider animal learning. They have provided an important text for psychologists, clinicians, counselors, and advanced students.

181. Lehane, Stephen. *Help Your Baby Learn: 100 Piaget-Based Activities for the First Two Years of Life.* Englewood Cliffs, N.J.: Prentice-Hall, 1976.

Designed for parents and caregivers, this volume provides many ways in which an infant's behavior may be understood and the child's environment enriched to facilitate development. There is space in the text to record each of a baby's developmental milestones.

182. Lickona, Thomas. *Raising Good Children.* *See* Chapter 3, item 131.

183. McCall, Robert B. *Infants: The New Knowledge.* New York: Random House, 1980.

McCall describes the capabilities of infants in their first years of life. He covers the ability of the newborn to see and hear their parents, their natural disposition toward getting to know their caregivers, and the growth of love and attachment between parent and baby. The author explores the changing mental abilities and social skills in the first and second years and advises the reader how to observe these stages. He also discusses the effect of early stimulation on a baby, how temperamental differences can forecast later personality, and whether it is possible to predict later IQ from infant tests. Among other topics of interest that he delves into are whether babies dream, which is better--breast or bottle feeding, when do parents start to feel love for their infants, and what kinds of toys infants enjoy.

184. McDiarmid, N. *Loving and Learning.* New York: Harcourt Brace Jovanovich, 1975.

This informative book works from the thesis that a loving relationship between parent and child sets the foundation for optimal growth and development. Developmental patterns are described along with activities for parent and child to share. Parents interested in making their own playthings will find this book a great help, as will all adults working or living with babies and toddlers.

185. McWilliams, Margaret. *Nutrition for the Growing Years.* *See* Chapter 2, item 67.

186. Marzollo, Jean. *Supertot: Creative Learning Activities for Children 1-3.* *See* Chapter 8, item 365.

187. Marzollo, Jean, and Janice Lloyd. *Learning Through Play.* *See* Chapter 8, item 366.

188. Maxim, George W. *The Sourcebook: Activities to Enrich Programs for Infants and Young Children.* Belmont, Calif.: Wadsworth, 1981.

Maxim's book contains a variety of activities for promoting development during infancy and the early years. Activities are designed to facilitate physical, intellectual, and language growth. Academic skills and creative and cooking activities are provided for toddler and preschool youngsters. There are also guidelines for observing early care/education programs.

189. Maxim, George W. *The Very Young: Guiding Children from Infancy Through the Early Years.* Belmont, Calif.: Wadsworth, 1980.

Theories of early education and development are comprehensively described. Maxim also has guidelines for programming in the areas of social-emotional development, values clarification, motor development, health and safety education, cognitive growth, academic skills, language development, science and social studies education, creative expression, and parent involvement.

190. Moore, Shirley G., and Catherine R. Cooper, eds. *The Young Child.* Reviews of Research, Vol. 3. *See* Chapter 3, item 138.

191. Munger, Evelyn M. *Childplay: Activities for Your Child's First Three Years.* *See* Chapter 8, item 369.

192. Neser, Gwen, and Janna Gaughan. *Infantoddler Parenting: Activities for Child with Adult.* *See* Chapter 8, item 370.

193. Osofsky, Joy D., ed. *Handbook of Infant Development.* New York: Wiley, 1978.

Osofsky has assembled articles and essays by some of
the most highly recognized experts in the field of infant development. There are suggestions for future
directions in infant research.

194. Painter, Genevieve. *Teach Your Baby.* New York: Simon
& Schuster, 1982.

Written for parents, this book offers an effective
step-by-step program of daily activities designed to
foster learning for every stage of development—right
from the start. The activities are grouped to match
the growth rate of infants, and each chapter gives
descriptions of toys and other learning materials to
help in the planning of daily educational play.

195. Piaget, Jean. *The Origins of Intelligence in Children.*
New York: International Universities Press, 1952.

This is a classic work describing the six substages of
the sensory motor period of development. Piaget utilizes
observations of his own children to illustrate the very
earliest phases of child development.

196. Richards, M. *Infancy: World of the Newborn.* See Chapter 3, item 143.

197. Salk, Lee. *The Complete Dr. Salk: An A-to-Z Guide to
Raising Your Child.* See Chapter 3, item 147.

198. Sattler, J.M. *Assessment of Children's Intelligence
and Special Abilities,* 2nd ed. Boston: Allyn and
Bacon, 1982.

This annotated directory of standardized and other
test measures for all ages of children is designed to
aid persons responsible for test selection, administration, and assessment.

199. Scheffler, Hannah Nuba, ed. *Resources for Early Childhood: An Annotated Bibliography and Guide for Educators, Librarians, Health Care Professionals, and
Parents.* See Chapter 7, item 327.

200. Segal, Julius, and Zelda Segal. *Growing Up Smart and
Happy.* See Chapter 3, item 150.

201. Smart, Mollie S., and Russell C. Smart. *Infants: Development and Relationships,* 2nd ed. See Chapter 3,
item 153.

202. Sponseller, Doris, ed. *Play as a Learning Medium.* *See* Chapter 8, item 388.

203. Stone, L. Joseph, and Joseph Church. *Childhood and Adolescence: A Psychology of the Growing Person,* 5th ed. *See* Chapter 3, item 157.

204. Stone, L. Joseph, Henrietta T. Smith, and Lois B. Murphy, eds. *The Competent Infant: Research and Commentary.* New York: Basic Books, 1973.

     The volume represents a compilation of much of the early and still relevant research on infancy. Special sections are included on individuality in development, prenatal and perinatal development, capabilities of the newborn, development in year one, deprivation and enrichment, and social development.

205. Walters, C. Etta, ed. *Mother-Infant Interaction.* *See* Chapter 3, item 161.

206. Weininger, Otto. *Play and Education: The Basic Tool to Early Childhood Learning.* *See* Chapter 8, item 390.

5

LANGUAGE DEVELOPMENT DURING INFANCY

Deborah Lovitky Sheiman

How much language do infants understand? Are babies expressing intention in their utterances? How does language
develop? What factors facilitate or impair it? Questions
such as these are central to the study of language development
and speech acquisition.

All youngsters experience a sequential pattern of language
development. The first cry is present at birth, and within
weeks the sounds of cooing appear. Coo's give way to babbling,
and soon the baby's vocalizations begin to resemble word
sounds. A connection of sounds with objects and actions takes
place. As the toddler stockpiles a vocabulary, he learns
there are rules to follow and specific exceptions to the
rules of his language.

Where do the roots of language production lie? Child
development experts agree that between 12 and 18 months most
children will begin to use language. However, months before
articulating that important first word the child has begun the
job of learning language. Through the babbling repetition of
syllables, infants reproduce and play with the sounds they can
make. Until approximately the ninth month of life, all infant
babblings sound alike. This occurs regardless of the language
to which the child is exposed. After this period the baby begins to shed particular sounds. He focuses on those sounds
that distinguish his language. For example, the German child
would repeat more guttural sounds, while an English child would
exclude these same sounds from his babblings.

Children comprehend the components of language before they
are able to express words. As early as 10 months of age,
babies are able to understand many of the words and expressions
of their language. Though the actual articulation of their
understanding remains months away, the baby can interpret ges-
tural cues and words from their context. It is during this
same period that babies shorten their vocalizations. "baba"
becomes "ba." Intonation takes on a language-like quality,

and sounds are uttered in a relatively appropriate context.
Parents delight in the idea that their baby makes sounds that
approach speaking.
    These new sound sequences that replace babbling convey a
purpose. One particular sound may signal anger or happiness,
while another will be used as a means of acquiring a goal.
One example is the infant who employs a specific sound while
looking toward a toy or caregiver in an attempt to indicate
a desire for the toy or caregiver's attention. Another is
the infant who is conveying joy with the same shriek of excitement each time mother enters the room.
    Linguists call these same repeated sounds "grouping ex-
pressions." They mark the baby's attempts at effective, indicating, and instrumental expression. Without the context
of communication and environmental cues, these grouping expressions would not be understandable.
    Language researchers have found that many of the baby's
first words are general nominals, such as ball, cookie, and
dog. Research on the structure of learning to speak has found
that the majority of these first word nominals represent the
names of objects that the baby acts upon. This suggests that
children pay little attention to objects and items that simply
exist. They focus on objects that do something, such as make
noise or move. This action is important to baby. It results
in novelty. Novelty attracts the child's attention.
    Baby's clearly understandable first words are, therefore,
usually coupled with an action. To illustrate this concept,
imagine a very young child vocalizing the word "ball" while
rolling it across the floor. Babies combine these first word
utterances, called "holophrases" with gestures, actions, and
facial expressions to communicate their needs and wants to the
outside world.
    Limitations exist in the baby's speech production. The
baby is restricted to the phonetic sounds and combinations he
is able to form. Consonants, where the tongue is positioned
in the front of the mouth, generally appear in baby's first
words. These include the consonants of P, B, T, and M. The
also easily formed vowel sounds of A and E appear frequently.
    Baby's first words frequently follow a pattern of conso-
nant-vowel, vowel-consonant, or consonant-vowel-consonant.
Words in this early period of speech are generally reduced in
form. The color red would sound like "reh." To the listener,
cup and up might be interchangeable. Though these initial
words are not perfect executions of adult speech, they are
adequate for parents to understand within the context of the
situation.
    Sound clusters, which are groups of two or more syllables,
enter the baby's speech repertoire around 18 months to 2 years.

The baby shortens these sounds for ease of production. The word "kitty" might be uttered as "itty" or "fork" as "ork." Multisyllabic words can prove to be difficult for the young child. Awareness of the different syllables may extend beyond the baby's ability to produce them.

Repetition of one syllable in a two-syllable word is common, as is the tendency to make all vowels or consonants in a word sound alike. One frequently hears a toddler ask for "ba ba," meaning bottle. Doggy may sound like "doddy." As the child repeats and combines familiar speech sounds, his lengthened utterances take on the characteristic sounds of his native language.

Early understanding of vocabulary develops rapidly. By age 2, most children understand about 250 words. The actual articulation of these words, however, develops at a more gradual pace. At approximately 15 months to 2 years, the child enters the naming stage. These names include items such as food, toys, and animals. Basic groupings of nouns appear first. One basic noun can have many uses, and a single word can stand for an entire sentence. A toddler's utterance of "up" can mean "pick me up" or "look at the sky." Baby's early words convey much more than perceptual characteristics of "up" can mean "pick me up" or "look up at the sky." Baby's all animals. This is referred to as an overextension.

Underextensions also crop up in the young child's language structure. The pet cat may be the one and only feline acknowledged by the child as being a "cat." Other cats and kittens on his block may be look-a-likes but to the child they are of another species.

Around 24 months the child will take first steps toward speaking in sentences. These early constructions are no more than simple word combinations. They are limited to the immediate, the here and now. They comment on actions and name objects. These expressions can relate information pertaining to possession or location. While attempts such as "me go" or "baby cry" lack the quality of adult speech, they permit the child expression of thought.

Receptive language, the ability to comprehend language, continues to surpass expressive language, the ability to communicate through speech. This early form of language is referred to as telepathic. Connecting words and articles are absent from the child's sentences.

Linguists suggest a hypothesis to explain this stage of language development. They note that the very young child is able to remember only that which is most important to the message. In most communications that would be the object, action, and agent.

Intonation, modulation of voice, and word stress are clues to the child's wants and meaning. Word stress and intonation can change a name to a question or request. Depending on the way a child utters the words "ball-play" can determine the meaning as "Can we play ball?" or "That's a ball to play with." Generalizations can be made as to the child's meanings. Most frequently it is the stressed word that adds new information to the communication. To illustrate, in most verb-location utterances, it is the location that is usually stressed-- "Go home?" In modifier-noun expressions, the modifier is likely to be the focus--"Big girl." This indicates that the young child is developing the skills necessary for conversation, in addition to a sense of sentence structure.

From two to three years of age, the development of syntax occurs. Syntax represents the ways in which words are put together to form phrases, clauses, or sentences. Linguists are not in agreement as to the course and nature of the child's word combinations and grammar.

One theory of grammar proposes the division of words into pivot and open classes. A pivot word usually begins a sentence. A pivot word cannot appear alone or with another pivot word. After the initial pivot word a string of possible open-class words follow. Open-class words can appear alone or with a pivot word. They constitute the largest part of the child's vocabulary. "More cookie" illustrates the pivot-open form. This theory of children's grammar is criticized for emphasizing structural consistencies while ignoring the meanings of word combinations.

The theory of case grammar accounts for meanings of word combinations. Case grammar is built upon case relations. These are universal concepts that distinguish and define who did what to whom. This theory hypothesizes that children's early language structures can be broken down into categories according to their relationships. Categories include the agent, which is the initiator of an action; an instrument, which is the object through which an action is performed; an experiencer, who receives the action; and a locative, which denotes where the action or state is happening. Case grammar accommodates the patterns and variations in language development.

The two-to-three-year-old child manifests the progression of syntax with pronouns, prepositions, articles, and auxiliary words. As the youngster advances from two-word sentences to longer expressions, inflection on the end of words is acquired. Inflections are usually suffixes. They add information on plurality (s), possession ('s), and tense (ed, ing).

Present progressive verb form, which denotes ongoing action, is generally first to emerge. "I going" illustrates this. The prepositions "in" and "on" mark location and appear

next. These are followed by the plural marker (s), irregular
past tense, possessive tense ('s), and the extension of the
word "no." To the toddler, "no" can mean nonexistence, re-
jection of an offer, and/or denial of a statement. In short
two-to-three-word sentences, the child places the negative
first, such as "no milk." As sentences expand in length to
four words, there is a tendency for the child to insert the
negative between subject and verb--"I no want apple."

Interestingly, negatives such as "don't" and "won't"
emerge before the positive "do" and "will." It is doubtful
that a young child divides "don't" into "do not." "Don't"
is understood as a whole single negative word.

In the three-word sentence, the young child begins to insert adjectives. The child moves from global, general adjectives (big) to more precise dimensional adjectives (long,
short). Negative adjectives are manifest after positive adjectives, and "less" shows up after "more" is already in the
vocabulary.

Also, between two and three years of age, the question
that was signaled by a declarative sentence with a rising
intonation on the end, gives way to more mature forms.
Auxiliary verbs are introduced into the child's vocabulary,
and the auxiliary verb and subject reverse to form a grammatically sound question "Can doggie play?"

"Wh" words enter the child's vocabulary. Where, what,
who, why, and when may be asked with endless repetition. The
progression of "wh" questions is not dissimilar to the structure
of question development in general. The declarative form appears first, followed by reversal of subject and verb. For
example, "Where go dog?" would emerge before "Where dog go?"

At approximately three years, children begin to retell
events that have occurred by using linking conjunctions. A
two-minute story about a trip to the store might sound like a
long, run-on sentence, as one idea is linked to the next with
the word "and." This form is known as a coordinate sentence.

By the time three years is reached, the child is generally
capable of carrying on a conversation that focuses on a common
topic and grammatically fits into the structure of the language
spoken.

Up to now, this discussion has focused on the child's
maturational development of language. Little comment has been
made on the role of the parent/caregiver in facilitating the
child's development of speech.

Research has suggested that parents do little to modify
the grammatical errors of their young child's speech. In contrast, focus is placed on the content of what the child utters.
Caregivers modify their speech to young children. They repeat
the initial sounds of the infant and the nouns that the toddler

has mastered. They use short, simple sentences and repeat
for emphasis. Exaggerated intonations and overuse of the
words the child has recently acquired are common.

This form of speech modification is called "motherese"
or "baby talk." Is this a helpful or harmful syndrome for
the baby? The shorter utterances used may assist comprehension since the memory of the young is limited to the immediate.
Simplifying sentence length and structure can assist the child
in selecting the salient words in each utterance. However,
simplification down to the actual level of the child can prove
harmful. Caregivers can provide motivation and encouragement
by providing examples for children that are slightly ahead of
their stage of development. Caregiver responsiveness to the
child's attempts at language are important for the child's
sense of competency. Simple recasts of the child's utterances
can provide an enthusiastic response, confirm what has been
said, and check the child's comprehension of the words used.

Language spoken in the home may differ from that spoken
in the child-care center or society in general. This creates
a situation where the child becomes bilingual. He grows up
speaking more than one language. Until recently, a child
with this experience was thought to be linguistically handicapped, not having the full exposure and development of one
language before another is acquired. Current research suggests that a child is capable of acquiring different languages
simultaneously.

Typically, each language is heard from a different source.
The primary language is spoken by members of the family, and
the secondary language stems from outside the home. The child
learns the distinct languages at different times, or in different situations, or from different sources. The child
learns to respond to both languages as a means of communi-
cating.

It should be remembered, however, that young children
usually are not equally proficient in both languages. The
amount of time the child is exposed to the language will affect proficiency and dominancy. The age at which the child
begins to speak, cognitive development, and verbal fluency
are not affected by bilingualism. Regardless of these factors,
the actual number of words in a bilingual child's vocabulary
is found to be smaller throughout the early years. This appears to be a meager loss for the acquisition of a lifelong
competency in a second language.

Through the previous pages this discussion has focused on
language acquisition and its complexities. Additionally,
speech and language have been viewed from a social-cultural
standpoint. In the 1800s a famous author, Ernest Dowson, asked
"What is the use of speech?" Now, over 100 years later, we can
simply answer "to communicate."

BIBLIOGRAPHY

207. Adler, Sol, et al., eds. *Lesson Plans for the Infant and Toddler: A Sequential Oral Communications Program for Clinicians and Teachers.* See Chapter 4, item 167.

208. Adler, Sol. *Poverty Children and Their Language: Implications for Teaching and Treating.* Orlando, Fla.: Academic Press, 1979.

This book was designed to be an introductory text, addressed to a broad spectrum of professional workers (including speech/language clinicians) and teachers (preschool, Head Start, early education, secondary education, remedial reading, and bilingual teachers). The intent is to alter the attitude of the middle-class professional worker toward the economically deprived child. Its fundamental premise is that conventional programming for the underprivileged child has failed in its mission to lead the child to the "American Dream"--a better life. The poor child still remains poor and undereducated. The book offers a different strategy--one with an enhanced understanding and use of the child's native mores, values, and dialect, while at the same time enriching the child's understanding of and ability to function in establishment culture.

209. Anistasiow, Nicholas J., and Michael L. Hanes. *Language Patterns of Poverty Children.* Springfield, Ill.: Thomas, 1976.

The authors discuss environmental influences on language development, language development stimulation, and its implications for bilingual education, as well as other topics relevant to the language of poverty children.

210. Beck, M. Susan. *Baby Talk: How Your Child Learns to Speak.* New York: New American Library, 1979.

For the reader without previous background in the field, this guide explains the way children deal with language. A comfortable blend of theory and practical application, the volume suggests how a child's innate capacity to learn language can be enhanced by environmental nurturing.

211. Beck, M. Susan. *Kidspeak: How Your Child Develops Language Skills.* New York: New American Library, 1982.

The sequel to *Baby Talk* traces the process by which
children learn the components of language.   Here the
focus is on how children discover that language has meanings, double meanings, and subtleties and thereby acquire the skills needed to understand riddles, tell
stories, and make up metaphors.   There is a brief, annotated bibliography.

212.   Bloom, Lois, ed. *Readings in Language Development*.
       Communication Disorders Series.   New York: Wiley,
       1978.

       The text is written primarily for researchers and
       clinicians.   Its collection of data is a synthesis of
       findings in normal language development.   Included are
       guidelines with a practical approach to the evaluation
       and management of children with language disorders.

213.   Bullowa, Margaret, ed. *Before Speech*.   New York: Cam-
       bridge University Press, 1979.

       This text is based on research in prelinguistic com-
       munication and the beginning of interpersonal communica-
       tion.   The material draws widely on research by scholars
       whose varied backgrounds have brought them directly and
       indirectly to the exploration of questions that bear on
       communication in the earliest phase of human infancy.

214.   Clark, Herbert, and Eve V. Clark.   *Psychology and Lan-
       guage: An Introduction to Psycholinguistics*.   New
       York: Harcourt Brace Jovanovich, 1977.

       The authors explore listening and speaking and the
       acquisition of these two skills by children.   Organized
       into five parts around these processes, the text traces
       listening from the initial perception to speaking and
       the relationship of language to thought.   The volume is
       designed for undergraduate and graduate students in
       psychology, linguistics, and related fields.

215.   Cruttenden, Alan.   *Language in Infancy and Childhood:
       A Linguistic Introduction to Language Acquisiiton*.
       New York: St. Martin's, 1979.

       This introductory textbook is primarily for students
       with some background in linguistics and phonetics, as
       well as for those concerned with language teaching or
       language remediation.   However, it is not concerned with
       how to teach.   The author's philosophy is that greater
       knowledge of the facts of language will enable teachers

and therapists to formulate their own tactics, and Cruttenden presents the linguistic facts of language acquisition in as theoretically neutral a way as possible. The book is fairly heavily referenced because it is intended as a guide for a more in-depth study of particular topics. Each chapter is more or less self-sufficient, so that students interested in only one aspect of the subject may read only the relevant chapter or chapters.

216. Dale, Phillip S. *Language Development: Structure and Function*, 2nd ed. New York: Holt, Rinehart and Winston, 1976.

Research findings that Dale has included in this technical reference have led to some fundamental changes in how professionals view the process of language development.

217. Deutsch, W. *The Child's Construction of Language*. Orlando, Fla.: Academic Press, 1982.

Deutsch discusses the child's role in moving up from early speech to patterns of speech that meet community standards. Acquisition of languages, other than, but including, English, is addressed.

218. DeVilliers, Peter A., and Jill G. DeVilliers. *Early Language*. Cambridge: Harvard University Press, 1979.

According to the authors, the "main purpose of this survey is to give some idea of the variety and scope of efforts to explore the language of the developing child." Through use of examples, the child's language acquisition process is described, showing how normal learning takes place and how problems can arise. The authors also investigate the problems that can arise from deafness, dysphasia, and autism. Written in non-technical terms, this book provides rich information for parents and professionals.

219. Feagans, Lynne, and Catherine Garvey. *The Origins and Growth of Communication*. Norwood, N.J.: Ablex, 1984.

Feagans and Garvey describe communication development in the child from the stages of infancy through early childhood. Their main theme is that communications is of central importance to individual development, as well as to interpersonal relationships. Their volume is targeted at the communications, language, or child development professional.

220. Genishi, Celia, and Ann Dyson. *Language Assessment in the Early Years.* Norwood, N.J.: Ablex, 1984.

An effort is made to help parents and teachers understand, encourage, and assess language development. Examples of children's language with adults and peers helps the reader to understand the developmental and sociolinguistic orientation of this book.

221. Hopper, Robert, and Rita J. Naremore. *Children's Speech,* 2nd ed. New York: Harper & Row, 1978.

In this second edition, the authors have taken the research findings of the preceding five years and translated them into everyday language for students and those who work with young children. The text offers a sound and practical introduction to communication development. Also covered is the acquisition process in the areas of phonology, syntax, semantics, and pragmatics. Most chapters contain suggestions for further reading, along with some description of the material covered in these works.

222. Jeffree, Dorothy, and Margaret Skeffington. *Reading Is for Everyone: A Guide for Parents and Teachers of Exceptional Children.* See Chapter 10, item 461.

223. Kuczaj, S.A., and D. Palermo, eds. *Language Development.* Language, Thought and Culture, Vol. 2. Hillsdale, N.J.: Erlbaum, 1982.

Kuczaj deals with what are considered the primary questions concerning language development, such as how the child achieves communication competence, the role awareness plays in the language acquisition process, the functions that language serves, as well as many other important concerns related to the development of language. The text is very technical and primarily directed at scholars of language development.

224. Lee, D.M. *Children and Language: Reading and Writing, Talking and Listening.* Belmont, Calif.: Wadsworth, 1979.

Although this book is meant primarily to assist teachers in helping children build their communications skills, those concerned with infant speech development will find much of value in Lee's presentation, particularly the first two sections on communication (the purpose of language) and oral communication (talking and listening). The first section sets the stage for effective communi-

cation by describing how meaning is conveyed and interpreted. It focuses on young children by examining
their thinking processes and the stages through which
language is developed.

225. McCall, Robert B. *Infants: The New Knowledge.* See
     Chapter 4, item 183.

226. Maxim, George W. *The Very Young: Guiding Children from
     Infancy Through the Early Years.* See Chapter 4, item
     189.

227. Moerk, E. *The Mother of Eve—As a First Language
     Teacher.* Norwood, N.J.: Ablex, 1983.

     Geared to the academic community, this volume explores
     first language acquisition. Emphasis is on the mother-
     child relationship. Described are mother's natural
     efforts to help children in language acquisition and
     mastery.

228. Moore, Shirley G., and Catherine R. Cooper, eds. *The
     Young Child.* Reviews of Research, Vol. 3. See Chapter
     3, item 138.

229. Nelson, Keith, ed. *Children's Language*, Vols. 1-4.
     New York: Halstead, 1978, Vol. 1, 1979, Vol. 2:
     Hillsdale, N.J.: 1982, Vol. 3, 1983, Vol. 4.

     This series combines current research with a reinter-
     pretation of the previous thinking and research in the
     field of language development. In their particular
     chapters the contributing authors offer an account of
     their area of expertise within the context of new ex-
     perimental contributions, review, and theory. Taken
     together, the volumes in this series provide significant
     unbraiding of prior, incomplete notions of the nature
     of children's language. The material is written for the
     professional and for those interested in language research
     and current data.

230. Pelligrini, Anthony, and Thomas D. Yawkey. *The Develop-
     ment of Oral and Written Language in Social Contexts.*
     Norwood, N.J.: Ablex, 1984.

     The authors focus on the interdependence of language
     and social context. Topics examined include language
     development through peer interaction. The text is
     written for researchers and language practitioners.

231. Pinker, Steven. *Language Learnability and Language
     Development.* Cambridge: Harvard University Press,
     1984.

     Pinker's landmark psychological study represents a new
     type of research in psycholinguistics and language de-
     velopment.

232. Pushaw, David R. *Teach Your Child to Talk: A Parent
     Guide.* Forest Grove, Ore.: International Scholarly
     Book Services, 1977.

     Pushaw's handbook is written to guide parents in
     having a direct and positive effect on their child's
     speech and language development. It is full of useful
     information, presented in an informal manner, with step-
     by-step instructions, and easy for the nonprofessional
     to grasp. The book will help a parent understand a
     child's general growth and development from birth to
     age five. Each chapter relates to a specific age, and
     the discussion is divided into three subsections: typical
     development for the period, questions of development,
     and suggested activities. The latter provide both
     variety and fun while helping a child to learn. In
     addition, Pushaw has a section entitled "If Your Child
     Has Special Needs."

233. Salk, Lee. *The Complete Dr. Salk: An A-to-Z Guide to
     Raising Your Child.* See Chapter 3, item 147.

234. Scheffler, Hannah Nuba, ed. *Resources for Early Child-
     hood: An Annotated Bibliography and Guide for Edu-
     cators, Librarians, Health Care Professionals, and
     Parents.* See Chapter 7, item 327.

235. Stone, L. Joseph, and Joseph Church. *Childhood and Ado-
     lescence: A Psychology of the Growing Person,* 5th ed.
     See Chapter 3, item 156.

236. Wood, B.S. *Children and Communication: Verbal and Non-
     verbal Language Development.* Englewood Cliffs, N.J.:
     Prentice-Hall, 1976.

     A practical source on how children learn to communi-
     cate effectively, this book is a complete and penetrating
     overview of the development of communication in children,
     including verbal, nonverbal, and pragmatic dimensions.
     Part 1 explores both the intrapersonal forces, such as

the biological and genetic, as well as the interpersonal forces, particularly the family, that affect a child's communication development. Part 2 uses contemporary research and theory in the field as it views the emergence of vocabulary, syntax, and semantics. Part 3 considers children's development of communication through their body language and voice. Part 4 presents a view of children's acquisition of communication competence. It explores the development of communication in five functional areas--controlling, sharing feelings, informing, ritualizing, and imagining.

6

THE EXCEPTIONAL INFANT

Kathleen Pullan Watkins

Among the thousands of infants born each year are many who by nature of physical or mental condition will require specialized care and attention throughout life. Some of these babies will gave impaired physical functioning, that is, they will be less able than other persons to move about or attend to physical needs without assistance. Those with mental impairment will experience lifelong difficulty with learning situations, making special schooling a necessity. Other children will be endowed with intellectual gifts or talents that will similarly require interest and cultivation by caring adults. These groups of children, the handicapped and the gifted, have something in common. Both require a unique blend of understanding and acceptance of the qualities that make them different in a world that strives for sameness.

Today, the term "exceptional" is used to describe any person whose educational needs are special, Most often, this includes individuals with visual, speech, hearing, language, and orthopedic impairments, as well as the gifted and talented. As preschool and school-agers these youngsters are entitled to receive appropriate schooling under Public Law 94-142, the Right to Education Act for Handicapped Children. However, the provision of special education addresses only one of the needs of children who must overcome many problems.

As is briefly discussed in the chapter on social-emotional development, the birth of a sick or handicapped infant can provoke trauma in a family. All parents hope for, perhaps even expect, that their offspring will be more attractive, more intelligent, and ultimately more successful than the children of others. Therefore, when an infant is born who temporarily or permanently is unable to fulfill parental expectations, mothers and fathers must make a difficult and painful adjustment. At first, there are emotional changes to deal with. Feelings of shock, guilt, anger, fear, and even a desire to run away from this crisis are not uncommon reactions. Even-

tually, parents must deal with a serious disruption to plans
for the future, sometimes being forced to accept that their
child will require lifelong care. When the new baby has siblings at home, attention is often diverted to and may remain
focused upon the infant whose special needs may permanently
alter family relationships. Many a young brother or sister
has difficulty understanding why parental time and energy
must be given to another.

These problems are made even more complex by society's
virtual abandonment of exceptional families. At a time when
needs for comfort and support are critical, financial burdens
are heavy, and child-caring hours are long and draining, many
in the community turn away in fear and uncertainty. Although
laws have been enacted that provide education and protect the
rights of exceptional persons, there is still much to be done
by way of changing public attitudes. The birth of an exceptional infant is not celebrated by family or community. Un-
sure of how to react or what to say, friends and neighbors
may remain distant, increasing the unhappiness and isolation
of the parents. It may well be this factor that contributes
to rates of child abuse and neglect, which are three to four
times higher for handicapped children than for their nonimpaired
peers. Despite higher instances of parenting disorders, many
parents of exceptional infants overcome their grief and rear
their children with love and tenderness.

When unemployment, language barriers, and educational
deficits are present, as they often are when families are
impoverished, survival issues tend to be the primary focus.
The birth of an impaired child places added stress upon couples
with limited resources who are already facing overwhelming
problems. Abandoned by society, the low-income family with
an exceptional infant may be forced to accept government support or charity programs in order to survive. In some cases
(such as one documented by the television news magazine "60
Minutes"), a family must institutionalize their handicapped
child in order to be eligible for financial assistance.
Parents are, thereby, discouraged from finding support in their
own community, from maintaining a degree of independence, and
perhaps most tragically, from preserving the family unit.
What is most baffling about such circumstances is that it is
often less expensive for parents of a handicapped child to
provide home care than it is for that same child to receive
full-time care in a residential facility.

It should be noted that some exceptional families are
the victims of illiteracy. That is, the inability to read
or write prevents some parents from learning of programs that
would directly benefit them and their child. In these cases,
families must rely upon word-of-mouth information, which is
not always the most reliable source.

It has already been established that exceptionality covers
a broad range of special needs, including various physical and
mental conditions. Samuel Kirk, respected spokesperson for
the special education field, has categorized exceptionality
as falling into one or more of the following general areas.
The term "communication disorders" refers to those impairments that affect speech and learning. The many types of
learning disabilities belong to this category, as well as all
manner of speech impediments, ranging from mild stuttering to
total nonverbalcy. Difficulties in communication may be a
unique problem or can be related to a primary impairment.
Cerebral palsy is an example of a disorder that can affect
speech.

Another group of exceptional infants have "sensory handicaps," including auditory or visual problems. Here again, the
range between mild and severe impairment can be great, and
identifying these problems in infancy is complicated by the
young baby's crossed, seemingly unfocused eyes, brief attention
span, and preverbal nature. It is often parental intuition
that plays a part in identifying a sensory handicap. When a
concerned parent notes that the infant seems not to be hearing
or seeing well and mentions this during a routine pediatric
exam, a physician has cause to take a closer look to assure
that sensory development is progressing normally.

A third classification of special needs is called "mental
deviations," that is, those children who are mentally retarded
and those who are intellectually gifted. The mentally retarded
are grouped together by IQ for purposes of special education
as educable, trainable, or severely and profoundly impaired.
The latter of these represents those children with the lowest
intellectual functioning. Mental retardation may be genetic in
origin, or can result from illness, brain injury, or maternal
or infant malnutrition.

On the other hand, giftedness is as little understood as
any form of exceptionality. A child may have academic gifts,
as in mathematics or science. Some children are identified as
"talented" when they show unique skills as a musician, writer,
performer, or artist. There are also youngsters whose language,
thinking, and leadership abilities set them apart from peers.
Occasionally, the gifted or talented child behaves so differently from the norm that identification is possible in infancy.
For the most part, however, unusual aptitude does not become
clearly apparent until school age.

The components of giftedness are some unique formula, the
main ingredients of which are heredity and environment. However, there are also unknown elements in genius, which have
evaded identification. There are some self-described "experts"
who would have parents believe that genius is little but genetic

engineering coupled with appropriate reinforcement. At this
time, however, there is little evidence to prove that giftedness can become a cottage industry managed by parents and
geneticists.

"Behavior disorders" are yet another division of exceptionality. This includes children with forms of emotional
disturbance or mental health problems. In some cases, abuse,
neglect, or other forms of trauma in infancy or early childhood may be at the root of behavior disorders. In other instances, children come from homes with loving, caring parents,
and the causes of emotional problems are unclear. Although
some behavior disorders remain undiagnosed in infancy, others
are apparent quite early due to extreme or deviant behaviors,
such as unusual aggression, withdrawal, or inability to separate from family members.

"Neurological and orthopedic impairments" are grouped
together due to the essential role of the brain in motor
functioning. Many physical handicaps are directly linked to
neurological malfunctioning. Much as a stroke or other brain
injury can cause permanent physical impairment, there are
other brain-to-muscle links in disorders such as epilepsy
and cerebral palsy. There are also physical handicaps that
are completely unrelated to the brain, such as those caused
by congenital malformation (an infant born without a limb, for
example) or those resulting from injury or necessary amputa-
tion.

There is also a category of exceptionality that includes
all children with "health impairments." These may be tem-
porary in nature, as when a child is recovering from illness,
or they may be both permanent and degenerative, impacting on
all aspects of a child's life. Sickle cell anemia, asthma,
congenital heart disease, and childhood cancers are examples
of chronic illnesses. These children require special physical
and emotional care, and even though activity may be limited,
they must be permitted the opportunity to experience life in
as normal a fashion as is possible.

For centuries, it was believed that handicapped children
were incapable of learning and without hope for success or
happiness in life. In the nineteenth century, Maria Montessori
made some of the first significant strides in demonstrating
the learning potential of the learning disabled and retarded,
and in the years that followed many innovative methods were
developed for teaching exceptional children. It has been
learned in recent years, however, that in order to maximize
the effectiveness of special education, early and accurate
diagnosis is essential.

Today, diagnosis of exceptionality is possible even before
birth through procedures such as amniocentesis and ultrasound.
Prevention of certain birth defects and inherited illnesses is

also possible via genetic counseling, in which the potential
for risk of a sick or handicapped infant is ascertained
through evaluation of a couple's genetic histories.

At birth, observation, measurement of length and weight,
and application of the Newborn Scoring System (Apgar test)
make it possible to detect certain health conditions immediately. The Apgar evaluates a neonate's respiration, appearance,
reflexes, and level of activity. It is not unusual for infants to be placed in a special-care nursery for several days
if there is any suspicion of a problem.

Observation of newborn health by parents and caregivers
is still the chief means of identifying infant health problems.
Those who know a baby best are most likely to notice unusual
behavior, problems with eating, sleeping, or elimination, or
developmental delay. Aided by regular pediatric examinations,
immunization against childhood diseases, and follow-up visits
for even minor health problems, other forms of exceptionality
can actually be prevented.

For both the mildly and severely handicapped infant, early
intervention is crucial. At times, intervention can be undertaken by the family with the recommendations and assistance
of health care personnel. Parents are advised to combine their
own capabilities and needs with the suggestions of specialists
in order to provide the best program for their baby. In the
most commonly utilized form of intervention, home care is combined with some form of infant stimulation, but before any
program can be effective, parent education must be undertaken.

There are four major steps in the process of educating
the parent of an exceptional infant. First, mothers and fathers
must be helped to deal with the emotions that follow the birth
of their special-needs baby. Although family adjustment may
take many months or even years, it is important that family
members accept an exceptional infant quickly. The first months
and years of life are so very important that valuable time may
be lost if parents fail to provide love and support to the
newborn.

Second, parents must be provided with as much accurate
information as they can digest about the nature of their
baby's condition and the prognosis for the future. Often information must be given gradually, and parents given many
chances to ask questions. Physicians, nurses, and social
workers are being sensitized to this and other issues surrounding the care of the exceptional family.

Third, parents must be apprised of their options with regard to services and programs available to assist them and
their baby. This process can begin in the hospital through
conferences with and referrals from social service personnel
and visits from special-needs agencies. Furthermore, parents

should be certain that the hospital pediatrician and the
physician who will care for their infant after discharge have
conferred while the baby is still in the intensive-care nursery. This action helps to assure that some source of guidance
and support will be available once parents are at home with
their infant.

Finally, in conjunction with their pediatrician and
specialists in the program they have selected for their baby,
parents should be helped to select the specific roles they
will play in infant development. Many good programs are un-
successful with individual children because the efforts of
teachers are not supported at home, perhaps because parents
feel unneeded or are unaware of their importance.

There are three major types of programs for exceptional
infants: parent-child programs, hospital programs, and developmental day-care programs. Parent-child programs focus most
directly on parent training. Using the infant's home as the
educational milieu, a parent educator works with parent and
child to support and strengthen basic caregiving skills and
provide materials and activities to meet baby's individual
needs.

A growing number of hospitals conduct day-care programs for
exceptional children. Providing comprehensive services, which
include nutrition, clinic care, physical therapy, social services, and infant stimulation as required by each infant,
these centers also mandate parent participation. Infants
with special needs may be referred to these programs by their
birth hospitals or referrals may instead come from private
diagnosticians or social service agencies. Hospital programs
are usually staffed by an interdisciplinary team of physical
and mental health, early childhood education, nutrition, and
social welfare personnel who are devoted to working along with
families in order to help children reach their potential.

Developmental day care combines comprehensive services
with child care to meet the needs of the exceptional child and
family. These programs may be provided in a center setting
or in a private home, and some operate 24 hours per day,
seven days per week to provide a respite for parents who are
overtaxed by child-rearing responsibilities. Unlike programs
that serve only those children with special needs, developmental day-care centers may provide a mainstream setting in
which handicapped, nonhandicapped, and gifted children participate together. Unfortunately, many of these centers are supported by federal funds, which means that admission is often
based upon income eligibility.

Intervention today is not always aimed at children with
previously identified handicaps. Many programs also serve
children who are at risk of developmental delay, child abuse,

or emotional disturbance for reasons of family problems, parent
health, or socioeconomic status.

One other type of intervention for infants with special
needs is the residential program. Once thought to be the only
option for severely handicapped or retarded infants, institu-
tionalization is now considered drastic and is adopted usually
when round-the-clock nursing care is required and the costs
of home care are prohibitive.

Since the 1975 passage of Public Law 94-142, there have
been measurable improvements in the quality of life for many
exceptional persons. This law provides that children with
special needs receive an educational program at no cost to
their families. This schooling must be appropriate to the
child's needs with respect to age, handicapping condition,
maturity, potential as demonstrated by past achievement, and
parental expectations. An individualized program must be
provided in a setting most suited to that youngster's learning
needs, called the "least restrictive environment." For some
children classes in the regular classroom are most beneficial,
while for others resource rooms, total special program, or day
school are the most effective sites for learning.

The educational needs of each child are determined through
the development of an individualized educational program, or
IEP. With input from an interdisciplinary team and the
youngster's parent(s), educational objectives most appropriate
to overall goals for the child are specified. Parents have
the right to disagree and to request a hearing if they feel
that their youngster's needs are not being met through the
program.

There has been much confusion relative to the provisions
of Public Law 94-142. Misunderstanding still exists regarding
the definition of "mainstreaming," with much of the public
and even some educators concerned that profoundly impaired and
multiply-handicapped children are propelled into regular class-
rooms with unprepared teachers. There have also been differences in the manner in which the law has been interpreted
from state to state. In some states, special education begins
at age 3 and ends formally at age 21, while in other regions
special services are available only from ages 6 to 18. It is
significant that in no state is special education mandated
during the critical years from birth to 3.

Yet another issue of significant concern is a financial
one. At the time of the passage of the Public Law, funding
for educational programs was plentiful and little thought was
given to the long-range source of monies to develop, staff,
and operate needed programs for exceptional children. Conse-
quently, many states have found it necessary in recent years
to enforce cutbacks in special education programs. As the

federal budget for education has little priority at present,
there are few offering practical solutions to current fiscal
difficulties.

What of the future and the roles of family, child advocates, and society in general in relation to the handicapped
infant? Some of the relevant issues have already been touched
upon, such as the exceptional family's great need for support
from the community. It is also evident that the private sec-
tor must assume a greater role in special education so that
established programs can both continue and grow. However,
advocacy is needed in other areas as well.

Public education for the prevention of all handicapping
conditions is essential. This means that existing programs
for genetic counseling, prenatal care, and research into the
causes of birth defects must be utilized and receive adequate
support.

The very early identification of infants with special
needs must be accomplished in order for children to take full
advantage of existing services. Health care, social service,
and education professionals play invaluable roles in this
process, but parents must liekwise be alerted to the signs
of developmental delay and other health problems.

Finally, there must be room made for exceptional infants
in existing day-care and developmental programs, whether or
not the law mandates admission. Only by exposing and rearing
all children in an environment free of prejudice toward the
handicapped, one that fosters understanding and acceptance of
individual differences, can the chances for equality of life
be maximized for all children.

BIBLIOGRAPHY

237. Alvino, Jamas, and *Gifted Children's Newsletter* Staff.
      *Parents' Guide to Raising a Gifted Child: Recognizing
      and Developing Your Child's Potential.* Boston: Little,
      Brown, 1985.

      Recent literature and research on gifted children is
      presented in a lucid and well-organized form. This is
      a valuable, practical guide for parents and profession-
      als on raising and educating gifted children.

238. Caldwell, Bettye M., and Donald J. Stedman, eds. *Infant
      Education: A Guide for Helping Handicapped Children
      in the First Three Years*. New York: Walker, 1977.

      In 1975 a group of leading infant educators presented
      papers on their work with disabled children under the
      age of three. This text grew out of these presentations
      read at the First Chance Network conference (San Antonio).
      Today, the findings are still relevant and important.

239. Colen, B.D. *Born at Risk*. New York: St. Martin's, 1981.

      Children at risk are defined as being born prematurely,
      weighting less than 5.5 pounds, or suffering from a
      congenital problem. Colen takes the reader inside the
      intensive-care nursery of a leading metropolitan hospital
      and presents a moving story about dedicated health pro-
      fessionals and the infants they fight to save.

240. Connor, Frances P., G. Gordon Williamson, and John M.
      Siepp. *Program Guide for Infants and Toddlers with
      Neuromotor and Other Developmental Disabilities*. New
      York and London: Teachers College Press, Columbia Uni-
      versity, 1978.

      In this collaborative effort, national in scope, ten
      years of work and experience in intervention for atypical
      children is recorded. Developed in cooperation with
      United Cerebral Palsey Association, the guide documents
      practical experience in program planning for children
      with disabilities. The authors suggest that while the
      programs are designed for team personnel, parents and
      other caregivers can gain better understanding of their
      child with special needs by reading the material.

241. Darby, Betty L., and Marcia J. May, eds. *Infant Assess-
      ment: Issues and Applications*. Washington, D.C.:
      Bureau of Education for the Handicapped, 1979.

      This comprehensive overview is based on papers pre-
      sented at two conferences sponsored by the Western States
      Technical Assistance Resource (WESTAR), 1978-1979.
      Severely handicapped infants are usually identifiable
      during the neonatal period. However, in mild or moderate
      conditions, the need for refined detection techniques is
      crucial for the establishment of an early identification
      of problems. Part 2 concentrates on intervention methods
      and programs. The book is recommended for paraprofession-
      als and professionals with a background in typical and
      atypical infant development.

242. Davis, W.F. *Educator's Resource Guide to Special Education*. Newton, Mass.: Allyn & Bacon, 1980.

    Davis describes the legislation, terminology, tests, and resources available to persons working in special education or mainstreamed settings.

243. Delahoyde, Melinda. *Fighting for Life: Defending the Newborn's Right to Live*. See Chapter 7, item 284.

244. Evans, J. *Working with Parents of Handicapped Children*. See Chapter 9, item 417.

245. Freeman, Roger K., and Susan C. Pescar. *Safe Delivery: Protecting Your Baby During High Risk Pregnancy*. See Chapter 7, item 291.

246. Harrison, Helen, and Ann Kositsky. *The Premature Baby Book: A Parent's Guide to Coping and Caring in the First Years*. New York: St. Martin's, 1983.

    Communicating with the neonatal team, emotional aspects of the birth crisis, medical problems are some of the topics dealt with in this supportive and helpful book. The authors include personal accounts by parents who had a premature baby, which makes for interesting and poignant reading. There is also a very useful appendix of resource organizations.

247. Jeffree, Dorothy, and Margaret Skeffington. *Reading Is for Everyone: A Guide for Parents and Teachers of Exceptional Children*. See Chapter 10, item 461.

248. Kranes, J.E. *The Hidden Handicaps*. New York: Simon & Schuster, 1980.

    Kranes furnishes guidance for parents and teachers working with youngsters who are marginally learning disabled. The use of tests for diagnosis and impact of learning disabilities on all phases of child development are discussed.

249. Lichtenstein, Robert, and Harry Ireton. *Preschool Screening: Identifying Young Children with Developmental and Educational Problems*. Orlando, Fla.: Grune & Stratton, 1984.

    The authors take the reader from an overview of preschool screening and early identification through practical considerations and recommendations. Their book is for practitioners, administrators, teachers, psychologists, and other professionals, as well as concerned parents.

250. Lyon, Jeff. *Playing God in the Nursery*. *See* Chapter 7, item 311.

251. Moore, Shirley G., and Catherine R. Cooper, eds. *The Young Child*. Reviews of Research, Vol. 3. *See* Chapter 3, item 138.

252. Nance, S. *Premature Babies: A Handbook for Parents*. New York: Arbor House, 1982.

One of the first volumes devoted exclusively to the special needs of the parents of prematures, Nance's book is designed to help parents feel at home in a neonatal intensive-care unit, to deal with common parental emotions, and to handle feeding and home-coming related problems. Readers will find a valuable glossary of terms related to a premature's health problems and a list of resources.

253. Nelson, Keith, ed. *Children's Language*, Vols. 1-4. *See* Chapter 5, item 229.

254. Newson, John, and Elizabeth Newson. *Toys and Playthings: In Development and Remediation*. *See* Chapter 8, item 371.

255. Ramey, C.T., and P.L. Trohanis, eds. *Finding and Educating High-Risk Handicapped Infants*. Baltimore: University Park Press, 1982.

The editors (based on their work with the Technical Assistance Development System, TADS), as well as the contributing authors, are pioneers in designing screening and intervention programs. They share their expertise in this book. The volume should be especially helpful to early childhood/special education students.

256. Safford, Phillip L. *Teaching Young Children with Special Needs*. St. Louis: Mosby, 1978.

Safford has organized his discussion around identified areas of special needs (including giftedness) of children from birth to eight years of age. He effectively combines theory with practical application and suggests how teachers as well as parents can provide in-

dividualized learning in the "least restrictive" environment. The extensive appendixes are designed to assist
with the assessment and testing of children.

257. Scheffler, Hannah Nuba, ed. *Resources for Early Child-*
      hood: An Annotated Bibliography and Guide for Educa-
      tors, Librarians, Health Care Professionals, and
      Parents. See Chapter 7, item 327.

258. *Special Hospital Care for Your New Baby.* Columbus, Ohio:
      Ross Laboratories, 1978.

      This is a helpful guide for the parents of infants in
      neonatal intensive care.

259. Stack, Jack M., ed. *The Special Infant: An Interdisci-*
      plinary Approach to the Optimal Development of In-
      fants. New York: Human Sciences Press, 1982.

      Stressing the interdisciplinary approach, this volume
      is an edited compilation of papers, workshops, and
      seminars presented at a conference of the Michigan Asso-
      ciation for Infant Mental Health. It should interest
      all professionals involved in the care and treatment of
      infants and young children.

260. Sugar, Max. *The Premature in Context.* New York: SP Medi-
      cal and Scientific Books, 1982.

      Sugar provides an update of the knowledge about the
      conditions, needs, and development of the premature
      baby.

261. Tingey-Michaelis, Carol. *Handicapped Infants and Chil-*
      dren. Baltimore: University Park Press, 1983.

      The author outlines situations that parents are likely
      to encounter in raising their handicapped child at home
      and offers sensitive and practical suggestions for meet-
      ing these special needs. For easy reference, he has
      organized the text in dictionary form with problems
      listed under general headings of feeding, health, sleep,
      syndromes, etc. The book is directed at parents but
      should also be useful to physicians and other health
      care professionals who work with disabled children.

ISSUES IN INFANT-FAMILY INTERACTION

Kathleen Pullan Watkins

In a world focused on lifestyles, careers, and material things, many young couples feel that their family is incomplete without a child. Seldom, however, do parents-to-be anticipate the changes that accompany this event, and surprised by the impact of becoming mothers and fathers, they find themselves evolving into unfamiliar persons with unexpected feelings and needs.

The changes that accompany the birth of a child actually begin with pregnancy. Although hormonal and obvious physical changes are unique to women at this time, expectant fathers often share the anticipation, excitement, and fear of the unknown experienced by their mates. Fathers-to-be also try to imagine the appearance, behavior, and future of their infant and are not immune to concerns that mother and newborn will come through the birth process safe and healthy.

Changes in birthing styles have once again made childbirth the family-centered experience it was prior to the advent of the maternity hospital and anesthesia. Today, parents may choose from a variety of childbirth preparation techniques which enable mothers to be alert and participating in their infant's delivery. Fathers are no longer routinely excluded from births but may be present as observers or coaches. Even those who prefer to pace the waiting room are helped to feel comfortable in the traditional paternal role. Women who choose to do so are encouraged to select a friend or relative to support them during labor and delivery.

The sterile look of the delivery room has also changed. Women can give birth in comfortable delivery suites with plants and curtained windows. Parents who select one of the new "birthing centers" deliver in a homelike atmosphere with family members in attendance.

It is not unusual for new families, following the birth of their baby, to be given private time in which to get acquainted. Many experts consider this period, called "nesting,"

essential to the earliest bonding processes. Rooming in and
early hospital discharge are also encouraged based upon the
state of maternal-infant health.

Unfortunately, there are many couples whose health or
genetic histories make childbearing impossible. Although advances have been made in overcoming some infertility problems,
there are still many couples who must turn to agencies to fill
the empty space in their family unit. While streamlined in
recent years, making adoption an option for both singles and
married persons, the adoption process is still drawn out and
frustrating. Persons desiring to adopt may wait months or
years for a child, and although prospective parents may state
preferences with regard to age, background, and health condition of their baby-to-be, there are few guarantees. The
complications of adoption serve very important functions,
however, assuring that those seeking children will be loving,
responsible parents.

Even before the adoption process is complete, many parents-
to-be express concern about when and what to tell their child
about how they came to be part of the family. For many years,
the accepted practice was to withhold such information during
childhood for fear that it would prove traumatic. Oftimes, a
child would then learn of the adoption accidentally. When
told in adolescence or adulthood, some adoptees feel anger or
betrayal. Most psychologists suggest introducing children to
the idea of adoption in early childhood, explaining about the
special place the child has filled in the family. As the
youngster becomes old enough to ask questions, especially
those about birth-parents, adoptive families should attempt
to answer these queries as frankly as possible.

Adoptive parents are sometimes plagued by fears about
their ability to parent successfully, secure the love of their
new child, and handle child-rearing crises. There is also the
birth-parents and the risk that the family that provided love
and care during the formative years will be abandoned by the
adoptee. While many adoptees eventually do seek out their
natural parents, few desire to leave behind the special relationships formed with their adopted family.

The arrival of a young baby in the family is both a joyous
event and a catalyst for change. First-time parents generally
experience these changes most dramatically, even when extensive
planning has taken place. Mothers and fathers with stable
work situations or hard-won careers may be required to set
aside professional goals temporarily. A carefully planned
family budget may be jarred by unexpected expenses. Most of
the changes experienced are, however, emotional ones. Many
couples without children have been accustomed to a degree of
freedom that is forfeit for child-care routines upon arrival

of the baby. There are decisions to be made about breast or bottle feeding and the sharing of new responsibilities. If the baby is not a first child, there may also be sibling rivalry to deal with. During the first two years, a family's life literally revolves around their infant, and for most parents, the new routine requires a tremendous adjustment and attempts to cope with many uncertainties.

Among the questions frequently raised by new parents is that of discipline or managing infant behavior. While discipline, per se, should not be a significant concern in the first year, some behavior problems do originate in infancy. Contrary to popular belief, however, such problems tend to begin with neglect rather than spoiling. In truth, it is difficult to spoil a young baby. Infant crying, for example, is most often generated by hunger, fear, or pain and should be responded to immediately. Although babies learn quickly that certain of their behaviors create a particular response in their parents, these children should not be thought of as manipulative or as merely attempting to get adult attention. Likewise, holding, carrying, touching, and stroking an infant should not be thought of as overindulgence. Instead, these parent-baby interactions play a critical part in social-emotional and cognitive learning.

Parents and caregivers should resist the temptation to put infants on adult-directed feeding and sleeping schedules, but should instead attend to baby needs as the infant indicates these exist. By three or four weeks of age, most newborns have developed a fairly predictable pattern of behavior, gradually becoming adapted to timetables similar to those followed by adults.

Most new parents find that a bassinet placed at their bedside is a nighttime aid in feeding and diapering, while it is also emotionally comforting to have the baby close by in the first weeks. At about three to six weeks, moving the infant to a nearby room gives parents a renewed sense of privacy and provides some relief from the immediacy of caregiving routines.

There is some controversy about permitting infants and young children to sleep with their parents on a regular basis. While some specialists feel that this provides children with a sense of security, others argue that it severely disrupts the privacy important for couples and may make children resistant to sleeping alone at a later point.

Birth of a second or third child can be the precursor of the common problem of sibling rivalry. It is not at all unusual for an older child to be uneasy about a new brother or sister. Newborns, after all, are made much of and attended to constantly by the adults around them. Older youngsters may need a great deal of reassurance that they are as important

and as loved as before the baby's arrival. Such assurances
must be more than verbal. Preparations for the infant should
begin before the birth and include any siblings. After mother
and baby are home, parents should try to spend time alone with
older children, plan special parent-child activities, and find
ways for siblings to participate in infant care. These steps
can greatly help to alleviate a youngster's concerns.

When sibling rivalry is a serious problem, the symptoms
are difficult to ignore. A child may become angry, with-
drawn, display sleeping or eating disorders, revert to infantile behavior, have problems in school, or even attempt to
harm the baby. Such extreme situations are rare, but when
they do occur, the advice of a youngster's teacher or pediatrician can be helpful. Most children quickly make the adjustment to a new brother or sister with the aid of parental
love and understanding. Infants, meanwhile, can benefit
enormously from affectionate interactions with their siblings.

Working parents are increasingly concerned about the issue
of "quality vs. quantity time" with their young children.
Assured by specialists that it is the nature rather than the
amount of time spent with their baby that is important, many
mothers and fathers still question the impact of long parent-
infant separations. They may feel deep anxiety about the
health and safety of their infant in their absence. In many
cases, even when cared for by a competent relative or professional caregiver, the parents' strong need to be with
their child is not assuaged. Mothers, in particular, may speak
of spells of depression and crying when work situations impel
them to leave their baby in the care of another. Despite the
trauma for parents, data from research consistently show
that if a baby receives high-quality day care while spending
parents' nonworking hours in a loving and supportive home environment, there is little chance for any ill effects on child
development.

In ideal situations, there are two parents to share child-
rearing responsibilities and quality time with a baby. Increasingly, however, there are more single, employed parents
who must be both mother and father to their infant. Although
in many single-parent families, adults balance their multiple
roles with comfort and success, others find rearing children
without a partner overwhelmingly fatiguing from both physical
and emotional standpoints. Both singles and couples rearing
children have been known to experience "parent burnout," a
syndrome associated with unrelieved stress and responsibility.
By some estimates, 50 percent of all parents suffer some of
the symptoms of burnout during the child-rearing years. It
is also suggested that stress is found equally among working
and nonworking parents, and pressure to be the ideal mother or

father beginning when one's child is an infant may be a contributing factor. There are an ever growing number of support groups for both single parents and couples designed to help families deal more effectively with stress. Interested parents can obtain information from local clinics, private pediatricians, colleges, schools, child-care centers, churches, and civic groups. It may also be helpful for young parents to know other nearby families with whom they can develop social relationships. One of the most important factors in parent burnout is a sense of isolation and lack of anyone with whom to share the emotional burdens of parenting.

One final note on this issue. All parents require private time during which they can get away from family responsibilities, as well as those associated with work or school situations. While vacations are not possible for all parents, mothers and fathers should assure that they have at least some personal time each day. No parent should feel that he or she is indispensable to the child. Such feelings can lead a child to develop a type of dependency that becomes emotionally unhealthy for adult and infant. Furthermore, despite declarations of love and caring, it is possible for a parent to come to resent a child-rearing situation from which there seems no relief.

During the past 20 years, there has been a growing interest in the role of fathering in the life of the infant. For centuries, Western culture accepted fathers as breadwinners with little influence upon their children during the formative years. Mothers were totally responsible for child rearing except under the most extreme circumstances, such as serious maternal illness or death. If widowed with young children, men turned over the care of their youngsters to female relatives or remarried quickly.

With the advent of the modern women's movement, new options opened up for men as well. For the first time, qualities seen as essential in the care and rearing of young children were emphasized as desirable masculine traits. Fathers could be tender, gentle, sensitive, and openly affectionate with their children. Today's males are expected to assume more than a cursory involvement with their children. Beginning with participation in childbirth, many share in all aspects of child rearing, and research has highlighted the role of fathers as primary attachment figures for their babies. Indeed, fathers are known to influence all aspects of child development. This recognition is welcomed by both men and women who believe that children need the love, support, and modeling of both mother and father.

It is not unusual for parents to speak of wanting "the
best" for their infant, often those things mother or father
themselves lacked as children. While an admirable goal, this
desire also has its difficulties. Young children can be
materially overindulged, and parents can impose their own
unfulfilled dreams on their children beginning in infancy.
In reality, what a baby needs is far less complex than most
people imagine--three simple gifts: unconditional love, unfail-
ing support, and recognition as an individual, rather than as
a carbon copy of mother or father. While these may seem
uncomplicated, they are among the most difficult skills of
responsible, loving parenting. They require that even in
infancy, parents accept their baby as an individual with unique
expressions, needs, likes, and dislikes. For from parent to
baby, a warm and loving home, quality parent-infant time,
gentle discipline, and a strong feeling of "family" shared
by mother, father, and children are "the best of everything."

BIBLIOGRAPHY

262. Ainsworth, Mary D., M.C. Blehar, E. Waters, and S. Wall.
      *Patterns of Attachment: A Psychological Study of the
      Strange Situation.* See Chapter 3, item 99.

263. Ashford, Janet Isaacs, ed. *The Whole Birth Catalog:
      A Sourcebook for Choices in Childbirth.* Trumansburg,
      N.Y.: Crossings Press, 1983.

      Encyclopedic in its scope, this catalog is basically
      a consumer guide to pregnancy, to birth, and on becoming
      a parent. There are reviews of books and articles, as
      well as descriptions of products, resources, and organi-
      zations. The lively style makes easy reading, and the
      information given should be of value to parents as well
      as professionals.

264. Baldwin, Rahima. *Special Delivery: The Complete Guide
      to Informed Birth.* Milbrae, Calif.: Les Femmes Publish-
      ing, 1979.

      Although the focus is on home birth, this comprehensive
      guide provides information about all aspects of preg-   nancy and birth. The author deals with questions about

the advantages as well as disadvantages of home birth, prenatal care, screening for risk factors, nutrition and exercise, birth preparation for delivery at home, complications and emergencies, care of the newborn, and post-delivery care of the mother. Couples are encouraged to reject the concept of birth as a medical procedure and to see it as a natural event for which they are ultimately responsible.

265. Belsky, Jay, et al. *The Child in the Family.* See Chapter 3, item 101.

266. Berezin, Nancy. *The Gentle Birth Book: A Practical Guide to Leboyer Family-Centered Delivery.* New York: Simon & Schuster, 1984.

The author reviews the historical, philosophical, and theoretical background to the Leboyer approach to childbirth. The focus is on showing in a variety of ways that having a baby need not be a dehumanizing experience detrimental to the well-being of both mother and infant.

267. Bert, Diana, et al. *Having a Baby.* New York: Delacorte, 1984.

Seven women present personal accounts about their pregnancy and childbirth experiences. They deal with such topics as smoking and drinking during pregnancy, depression, and when to return to work.

268. Bing, Elizabeth, and Libby Coleman. *Having a Baby After Thirty.* New York: Bantam, 1980.

There has been a definite shift toward delayed childbearing in the United States since the 1960s. Bing and Coleman address the special problems and concerns of childbearing from the perspective of the woman over thirty.

269. Bode, Janet. *Kids Having Kids.* New York: Franklin Watts, 1980.

Within an introductory framework of teenage sexual conduct in cultural and historical terms, the author gives perspective to her discussion of contemporary practices. Areas considered include the special health risks connected with teenage pregnancy, abortion, adoption, and being a single parent. The tone is nondidactic, and the focus is on furnishing information that will enable young people to look at the possible choices and make informed decisions.

270. Bohannan, Paul. *All the Happy Families*. New York: McGraw-Hill, 1985.

    Looking through the eyes of an anthropologist, the author examines family life as it exists today. For Bohannan, it is not the man-woman relationship that makes up the core of the family. He suggests that it is the child who is in fact a pivotal part in the structure of family life. Interesting insights make this compelling reading.

271. Brazelton, T. Berry. *On Becoming a Family: The Growth of Attachment*. See Chapter 3, item 105.

272. Brewer, Gail, and Janice P. Greene. *Right from the Start: Meeting the Challenge of Mothering Your Unborn Baby*. See Chapter 2, item 37.

273. Browder, Sue. *The New Age Baby Name Book*. New York: Workman Publishing Company, 1978.

    Far from writing the traditional "name" book, Browder here gives the meanings and pronunciations of a great many heritage names from cultures all over the world-- African, Asian, East Indian, Russian, Latin and South American, etc.--as well as ecological and astrological names.

274. Brown, Catherine Caldwell, and Allen W. Gottfried. *Play Interactions: The Role of Toys and Parental Involvement in Children's Development*. Pediatric Round Table #11. See Chapter 8, item 349.

275. Clegg, Averil, and Anne Woollett. *Twins: From Conception to Five Years*. New York: Van Nostrand Reinhold, 1983.

    The authors have written a practical guide about every aspect of having twins, from conception, pregnancy, labor to the start of school. It is a supportive book that sensitively deals with the joys as well as the problems of caring for twins.

276. Close, Sylvia. *The Toddler and the New Baby*. See Chapter 3, item 107.

277. Cobb, John. *Babyshock: A Survival Guide for the New Mother*. Englewood Cliffs, N.J.: Prentice-Hall, 1983.

    While the father often feels left out with the arrival

of a new baby, a new mother too needs more attention
than she generally receives. Cobb addresses this problem by answering questions about the physical and emotional changes a new mother can expect, how to deal with
depression, lack of privacy, husband/wife relationships,
social life, vacations, and the myriad of other issues
that are likely to confront the parents.

278. Cohen, Jean-Pierre, and Roger Goirand. *Your Baby: Preg-
      nancy, Delivery, and Infant Care.* See Chapter 2, item
      41.

279. Cohen, Judith Blackfield. *Parenthood After 30?* Lexing-
      ton, Mass.: Heath, 1985.

      The physical, psychological, and social considerations
      of delayed parenthood are examined by the author, giving
      guidelines for those pondering this personal decision.
      In her discussion, Cohen considers the benefits and
      risks.

280. Cole, K.C. *What Only a Mother Can Tell You About Having
      a Baby.* New York: Berkley, 1983.

      Basing her discussion on research with first-time
      mothers, the author considers a wide range of phycologi-
      cal and physiological changes that come with having a
      baby. She also examines various birthing methods, hos-
      pitals, the changed lifestyle, traveling with a baby,
      and working.

281. *The Commonsense Guide to Birth and Babies.* By the Edi-
      tors of Time-Life Books. See Chapter 2, item 43.

282. *Consumer Guide,* Editors of. *The Complete Baby Book.*
      New York: Simon & Schuster, 1979.

      The new parent or parent-to-be will find this manual
      a complete guide to baby products, toys, medical services,
      health, and nutrition. There is also a national direc-
      tory of special help agencies and a directory of sources
      and manufacturers for the services and products in-
      cluded.

283. Curto, Josephine J. *How to Become a Single Parent: A
      Guide for Single People Considering Adoption or Natural
      Parenthood Alone.* Englewood Cliffs, N.J.: Prentice-
      Hall, 1983.

      While this book serves to encourage those who contemplate single parenthood, it also is designed to convince any single to assess his or her personal motivations realistically and carefully. From emotional and social factors to financial and legal considerations, the author, a single parent, has written a book that touches equally on the rewards and responsibilities of parenthood.

284. Delahoyde, Melinda. *Fighting for Life: Defending the Newborn's Right to Live.* Ann Arbor, Mich.: Servant Books, 1984.

Delahoyde asserts that in the United States some severely handicapped babies are permitted to die by having treatment denied to them. The reader is warned that unless we protect handicapped babies, infanticide will become "legalized."

285. Del Bo, L.M. *A Guide for the Future Mother: A Practical Medical Manual on Pregnancy, Childbirth, and Infant Care.* Englewood Cliffs, N.J.: Prentice-Hall, 1977.

Less concerned with psychological advice, Del Bo addresses much that has to do with the sexual life of women who are preparing to become wife and mother. Detailed information is given about the female and male reproductive systems, how fertilization occurs, how to have a healthy married life, and how to calculate the time of ovulation. A short history of the Lamaze Method is included, and there are step-by-step suggestions to use on the day of delivery, including ways to help with the delivery process. Information is also given on basic child care and how to cope with the possibility of postpartum depression.

286. Dick-Read, Grantly. *Childbirth Without Fear.* New York: Harper & Row, 1984.

A classic of natural childbirth, *Childbirth Without Fear* is a step-by-step guide for expectant parents, their teachers, and their attendants. The first section covers the principles of natural childbirth, including historical and religious influences, the conduct of labor, childbirth and the family, and childbirth in perspective. The second section discusses the practice of natural childbirth, including prenatal health, breathing, relaxation, labor, birth, care of the newborn, and the new mother. The third section goes into historic references for natural childbirth, and the final section covers the physiology of childbirth.

287. Draper, Henry E., and Wanda Draper. *The Caring Parent.*
     Peoria, Ill.: Bennett, 1983.

     This textbook is designed for teaching the subject of
     parenting in high schools and community colleges. As
     such, it is a good guide for students planning to use
     the information professionally or as parents. Supple-
     menting the text is a teacher's resource guide as well
     as a student guide with references, questions, and extra
     activities to help in the development of parenting
     skills.

288. Entwisle, Doris R., and Susan G. Doering. *The First
     Birth: A Family Turning Point.* Baltimore: Johns
     Hopkins University Press, 1981.

     As described by the authors, both social scientists,
     their primary purpose in writing this volume is to re-
     port the profound effect pregnancy and childbirth have
     on marital life, on family relationships, on the careers
     of the new parents, and on the children themselves.
     There is a detailed longitudinal study of 120 women and
     60 of their husbands around the time of the birth of
     their first child. Generally, the authors have provided
     a broad picture, with such topics as birth in American
     society, the course of pregnancy, birth event and early
     postpartum period, the couple's relationship, and early
     parenting. Family counselors, parents-to-be, teachers
     of childbirth preparation classes, students, and teachers
     in the social sciences will find this a useful reference.

289. Ewy, Donna, and Rodger Ewy. *Guide to Parenting: You and
     Your Newborn.* See Chapter 2, item 47.

290. Fitzpatrick, Jean Grasso. *Pregnancy and Work.* New York:
     Avon, 1984.

     With more and more women working while pregnant, Fitz-
     patrick hopes not only to help pregnant women survive
     the experience, but actually to enjoy it. Chapter topics
     include negotiation of maternity leaves from the job,
     occupational (and other) hazards, symptoms and how to
     cope with them, stress, nutrition, and how to look ter-
     rific while pregnant. There are guidelines for finan-
     cial planning, as well as all aspects of pregnancy, and
     baby care.

291. Freeman, Roger K., and Susan C. Pescar. *Safe Delivery:
     Protecting Your Baby During High Risk Pregnancy.* New
     York: Facts on File, 1982.

It seems that almost suddenly leaping advances have
been made in high-risk obstetrics (maternal-fetal medicine or perinatology) and neonatology (the specialized
care for sick newborn). In clear, sensitive terms, the
authors explain what high-risk pregnancy is and how the
problem is best managed. There is a detailed discussion
on the role of the doctor, selection of hospital, need
for specialized care, as well as functions of technologies
such as ultrasound, amniocentesis, the contraction stress
test, and fetal monitoring.

292. Gansberg, Judith, and Arthur P. Mostel. *The Second
     Nine Months: The Sexual and Emotional Concerns of the
     New Mother*. New York: Tribeca, 1984.

     What happens after the baby joins the family is the
     focus of this informative volume. Topics include bring-
     ing the new baby home from the hospital, coping with
     fatigue, breast feeding vs. bottle feeding, returning
     to work, as well as the special problems of single
     parenting.

293. Goldstein, Joseph, Anna Freud, and Albert J. Solnit.
     Before the Best Interests of the Child. New York:
     Free Press, 1980.

     In their earlier book, *Beyond the Best Interest of the
     Child*, the authors limited their inquiry mainly to prob-
     lems involving children already caught up in the legal
     system. Here they examine the conditions that would
     justify state intervention in family life. Challenging
     and authoritative, this work should be helpful to all
     who are committed to a humane and family-centered society.

294. Goldstein, Joseph, Anna Freud, and Albert J. Solnit.
     Beyond the Best Interests of the Child. New Edition
     with Epilogue. New York: Free Press, 1980.

     Now an established classic, this book has set new stan-
     dards in child placement disputes. The authors, two re-
     nowned psychologists and a well-known legal authority,
     spell out principles and criteria for deciding if separa-
     tion from the family and/or placement outside the home
     is best for a child's need for stability and continuity.

295. Greywolf, Elizabeth S. *The Single Mother's Handbook*.
     New York: Quill, 1984.

     According to the author, in the United States one
     child in five now lives in a single-parent home. Here

is a down-to-earth guide for single mothers to help
them cope with the child, as well as money, time, and
work-related situations. This work grew out of the
Stress and Families Project at Harvard University in
which women shared their experiences for the purpose
of making this practical handbook possible.

296. *Growing Parent: A Sourcebook for Families.* Editors of
   Growing Child/Growing Parent. Chicago: Contemporary
   Books, 1983.

   This thoughtful guide is designed to make parents more
   self-confident in their interaction with their child.
   It is not about the stages of child development. Rather
   it addresses concerns such as setting limits, coping
   with fussy, colicky babies, problem grandparents, and
   the spacing of children. It is excellent reading for
   both parents and professionals.

297. Haber, Michele Ingrassia, and Barbara Kantrowitz. *The
   Ultimate Baby Catalog.* New York: Workman Publishing,
   1982.

   From baby announcements that cost as much as $375 and
   Tiffany silver baby rattles for $90 to an ivory silk
   christening dress for $1000, this "ultimate" catalog
   is for parents who want their baby in "style" and can
   afford it. Readers will find information about cradles,
   layettes, toy chests, highchairs, playpens, books and
   toys, as well as a shopping list with some addresses
   from overseas.

298. Hannon, Sharon. *Childbirth: A Sourcebook for Conception
   Pregnancy, Birth, and the First Weeks of Life.* New
   York: Evans, 1980.

   For new parents, the author considers many parenting
   issues, among them the changing role of parenting, and
   gives advice on varied topics--for example parents'
   legal rights, photographing the delivery, and obtaining
   medical records.

299. Harrison, Helen, and Ann Kositsky. *The Premature Baby
   Book: A Parent's Guide to Coping and Caring in the
   First Years. See* Chapter 6, item 246.

300. Johnson & Johnson Baby Products Company. *The First
   Wondrous Year: You and Your Baby.* New York: Macmillan,
   1979.

Here is a complete compilation based on the research and experience of professionals and parents. It offers advice and insight into the problems and rewards of parenthood. It discusses dealing with "baby blues" and the changes a baby brings into a marriage. It gives advice on how to read and respond to cries and how to interpret your baby's physical and sensory skills: moving, touching, holding, seeing, hearing, and making sounds. There are also practical ideas about designing a nursery to choosing the best toys and a helpful section on games to play with your infant.

301. Kanter, Carol N. *And Baby Makes Three: Your Feelings and Needs as New Parents*. Minneapolis: Winston Press, 1983.

Becoming new parents is often a "mixed bag" of mixed feelings. Kanter deals with those dual feelings with supportive understanding and compassion.

302. Kitzinger, Sheila. *Birth at Home*. New York: Oxford University Press, 1979.

This book considers choices and alternatives. The author shows that having a baby at home can be a profoundly fulfilling experience, but she also talks about the possible risks, especially when risk factors known ahead of time preclude home birth. The role of the father as well as older siblings is touched on in this most informative treatment of the subject.

303. Klaus, Marshall H., and John H. Kennell. *Parent-Infant Bonding*, 2nd ed. *See* Chapter 3, item 124.

304. Korte, Diana, and Roberta Scaer. *A Good Birth, A Safe Birth: How to Ensure the Best Possible Birth for You and Your Baby*. New York: Bantam, 1984.

Even today's well-informed parents fail to examine the childbirth options open to them and settle for traditional medical care. Written by two La Leche League leaders, this book should be read by all expectant parents interested in learning about how to ask for and get the birth desired, when high-tech intervention is appropriate, how to choose a pediatrician, etc.

305. La Leche League International. *The Womanly Art of Breastfeeding*. *See* Chapter 2, item 60.

306. Lauersen, N. *Childbirth with Love: A Complete Guide to Fertility, Pregnancy and Childbirth for Caring Couples.* New York: Putnam, 1983.

   There is detailed material on all aspects of pregnancy and childbirth. Issues such as planning for pregnancy, infertility, conception, what to expect during pregnancy, genetic counseling, high-risk pregnancies, and complications of pregnancy are dealt with thoroughly. Other topics considered include the emotional life of the unborn child and the selection of an obstetrician.

307. Leach, Penelope. *Babyhood*, 2nd ed. *See* Chapter 1, item 15.

308. Leavenworth, Carol, et al. *Family Living.* Englewood Cliffs, N.J.: Prentice-Hall, 1985.

   This textbook, designed for junior high and high school students, covers a wide range of relevant information relating to family living. Many aspects of parenthood, child development, and child rearing are explored, with focus as well on family management, health, housing, and families in crisis. Each chapter opens with an overview and closes with a summary of the material presented. Included is a money management glossary and a listing of the effects and risks of drug abuse.

309. Lesko, Matthew, and Wendy Lesko. *The Maternity Sourcebook.* New York: Warner Books, 1984.

   Written by a husband and wife team, this comprehensive volume provides much information that should help resolve many of the major concerns about pregnancy, childbirth, and infant care.

310. Liman, Ellen. *Babyspace: A Guide for Families with Shrinking Space.* New York: Perigee, 1983.

   The central theme is "finding, furnishing, decorating, and equipping a place for your newborn that will grow with--rather than be outgrown by--your child." Finding the right space for that all-important room in the house is difficult even when money is not a problem. *Babyspace* is designed to help, with suggestions for creating a functional, creative, and economical babyspace. Chapters especially valuable discuss "Childproofing Your Home," "Privacy in a Shared Space," and "Stretching Babyspace."

311. Lyon, Jeff. *Playing God in the Nursery.* New York:
      Norton, 1985.

      Here is a compelling account of the legal, social,
      moral, scientific, and financial implications of de-
      cisions to withhold treatment from profoundly handicapped
      newborns. Lyon has written a well-researched book that
      deals sensitively with a topic that must be confronted.

312. Marzollo, Jean, comp. *9 Months, 1 Day, 1 Year: A Guide
      to Pregnancy, Birth and Babycare.* New York: Harper &
      Row, 1975.

      Written by parents for parents about real experiences
      during pregnancy, birth, and new parenthood, this book
      is a practical resource that answers, with sensitivity
      and reassurance, many questions new parents might have.

313. Maxim, George W. *The Very Young: Guiding Children from
      Infancy Through the Early Years.* See Chapter 4, item
      189.

314. Mayle, Peter. *How to Be a Pregnant Father: An Illus-
      trated Survival Guide for the First-Time Father.*
      Secaucus, N.J.: Lyle Stuart, 1977.

      Here is a light-hearted book, written by a father
      for fathers-to-be. Filled with sound advice from deal-
      ing with morning sickness to claiming maximum tax deduc-
      tions, it should be read by all expectant fathers (and
      mothers).

315. Meyer, Tamara. *Help Your Baby Build a Healthy Body: A
      New Exercise and Massage Program for the First Five
      Formative Years.* See Chapter 2, item 71.

316. Morrone, Wenda Wardell. *Pregnant While You Work.* New
      York: Macmillan, 1984.

      Pregnant women always had to learn how to cope with
      morning sickness, but today's pregnant woman may have
      to worry how to handle, additionally, a nine-o'clock
      board meeting. This book is all about balancing a
      career, a home, a husband, and a pregnancy.

317. Nance, S. *Premature Babies: A Handbook for Parents.*
      See Chapter 6, item 252.

318. North, A. Frederick. *Infant Care*, rev. ed. Washington,
      D.C.: U.S. Department of Health and Human Services,

Administration for Children, Youth, and Families, 1980.

This popular publication, along with *Prenatal Care* (equally popular), reflects the latest thinking of experts in the field. Both booklets are based on questions most frequently asked by pregnant women and those planning pregnancy. The suggestions offered are both sound and sensitive.

319. Odent, Michael. *Birth Reborn*. New York: Pantheon, 1984.

An internationally famous childbirth pioneer shares his revolutionary (perhaps controversial) childbirth methods, for the first time, with American readers. Dr. Odent depicts clearly what birth is like at his hospital, located in a small town in northern France. There women are free to give birth in any position that comes most natural to them. There are no drugs, and surgical intervention is used only in emergencies. The maternity unit reports some of the lowest problem rates and postpartum depression figures in the world, thus attesting to the success of Odent's methods.

320. *Our Baby ... Our Birth: A Manual for Prepared Childbirth*, 2nd ed. Ellie Shimer et al., eds. Wayne, N.J.: Avery, 1981.

Supporting all aspects of family-centered childbirth, this manual promotes the father's full participation in the pregnancy, labor, and birth process, as well as all practices that contribute to a safe childbirth and a warm and loving relationship between infant and parent.

321. *Photographing Your Baby*. By the Editors of Eastman Kodak Company. Reading, Mass.: Addison-Wesley, 1984.

Most parents want to capture the special, ephemeral moments in the new baby's life. Illustrated with delightful photographs, this book is a most helpful guide to baby picture taking.

322. Queenan, J. *A New Life: Pregnancy, Birth and Your Child's First Year*. New York: Van Nostrand Reinhold, 1979.

Queenan, Professor and Chairman of the Department of Obstetrics and Gynecology at the School of Medicine of the University of Louisville, offers an overview of

pregnancy, delivery, and the early growth and development of the child. Several of the chapters were con-
tributed by health care professionals. Topics include
fertility and conception, major and minor complaints in
pregnancy, the normal puerperium, the baby at home,
common problems in the newborn, development in the first
year, preventing accidents and a guide to your baby's
health. An interesting inclusion is the personal accounts from parents of their own experiences of pregnancy, the birth itself, and early parenthood. There
are also many instructive diagrams and photographs.

323.   Reich, William. *Children of the Future: On the Preven-
       tion of Sexual Pathology*. New York: Farrar Straus
       Giroux, 1984.

       In this compilation of writings that reach back to
       1928, Reich demonstrates through research findings the
       enormous impact of the environment on the infant. His
       ideas about the traumatic effect of birth on the infant
       are disturbing. The essays remain fresh and relevant,
       discussing early disturbances in children, infant mas-
       turbation, and parental attitudes toward childhood sex-
       uality.

324.   Ribble, Margaret A. *The Rights of Infants: Early Psycho-
       logical Needs and Their Satisfaction*, 2nd ed. New
       York: Signet, 1965.

       First published in 1943 by Columbia University Press,
       this book is still an important contribution to the
       literature. Addressed to "all inquiring parents," the
       author offers insights and effective ways for dealing
       with situations as they confront new parents. Ribble
       is mainly concerned with the emotional health of the
       infant, "the feeling life of a baby," a concern that,
       she feels, is often neglected.

325.   Richards, M. *Infancy: World of the Newborn*. *See* Chap-
       ter 3, item 143.

326.   Salk, Lee. *Your Child's First Year*, *See* Chapter 3,
       item 148.

327.   Scheffler, Hannah Nuba, ed. *Resources for Early Child-
       hood: An Annotated Bibliography and Guide for Educators,
       Librarians, Health Care Professionals, and Parents*.
       New York: Garland, 1983.

An outstanding overview of early childhood research, this comprehensive bibliography is useful to parents and professionals in every aspect of child care. An excellent chapter on resources, print and nonprint, concludes the volume.

328. Schrotenboer, Kathryn, and Joan Solomon Weiss. *Dr. Kathryn Schrotenboer's Guide to Pregnancy over 35.* New York: Ballantine, 1985.

Many of the fears and misconceptions connected with over-35 pregnancy are examined and alleviated. Practical guidelines take the expectant mother through every stage of concern. The book also helps deal with the emotional side of pregnancy.

329. *Selected Annotated Bibliography on Black Families, A.* Washington, D.C.: U.S. Department of Health, Education and Welfare, 1978.

This government publication provides an annotated bibliography of books related to issues in the lives of black families, such as family characteristics, the role of the child welfare system in family life, and social welfare services.

330. Simkin, P. *Pregnancy, Childbirth and the Newborn.* Deephaven, Minn.: Meadowbrook Press, 1984.

In this comprehensive volume one will find helpful information on prenatal care, nutrition during pregnancy, exercises for the expectant mother, labor preparation, birth, postpartum care, caring for the newborn, and the physical and emotional adjustments in the immediate weeks after childbirth. In addition, expectant parents will learn what happens to the fetus, the mother, and even to themselves during each trimester of pregnancy, what warning signs to look for, what fetal tests are available, vitamins and medication to be taken, and much more. Illustrations, charts, and tables supplement the text. Advice is also given on interviewing an obstetrician or midwife and selecting a childbirth preparation class.

331. Spock, Benjamin. *Raising Children in a Difficult Time.* New York: Pocket Books, 1974.

Some parents believe in raising their children with overpermissiveness, some with sternness. Dr. Spock believes that children "grow up behaving well and responsibly primarily because they love the parents who have loved them." In this book he also shares his thoughts on character development, fostering good attitudes in children, teaching beliefs and ideals, the role of grandparents, and the changing family.

332. Spock, Benjamin, and Michael B. Rothenberg. *Dr. Spock's Baby and Child Care*. New York: Pocket Books, 1985.

For several generations, *Baby and Child Care* has been, and continues to be, the most reliable sourcebook for parents. In this edition, writing with pediatrician and child psychiatrists Dr. Michael B. Rothenberg, Dr. Spock has updated his work by including information and advice on alternative birthing methods; day care centers; working mothers; role of fathers; "superkids"; divorce, custody and single parenting. All of Dr. Spock's time-tested advice (on health, nutrition, development ...) is here alongside the guidance to help parents meet the challenging world of the eighties.

333. Stevens, Joseph H., Jr., and Marilyn Mathews, eds. *Mother/Child, Father/Child Relationships*. Washington, D.C.: National Association for the Education of Young Children, 1978.

The aim of the authors was to include research that promised to have the greatest impact on the work of practitioners who counsel parents. The reports selected are of seminal nature touching on such questions as parental roles, how societal changes affect the family, the effects of alternative family styles on children, minority families, and parent-to-infant attachment. One chapter examines critically some research methods, especially direct observation of the caregiver and the child in natural day-to-day contexts.

334. Stone, L. Joseph, and Joseph Church. *Childhood and Adolescence: A Psychology of the Growing Person*, 5th ed. *See* Chapter 3, item 156.

335. Stoutberg, Susan Schiffer. *Pregnancy Nine to Five: The Career Woman's Guide to Pregnancy and Motherhood*. New York: Simon & Schuster, 1985.

There is a wide range of topics in this useful guide, for example, how to look good and feel good on the job, travel during pregnancy, and child-care arrangements. Of special interest are brief profiles of well-known women who successfully combine motherhood and career.

336. Tingey-Michaelis, Carol. *Handicapped Infants and Children.* See Chapter 6, item 261.

337. Verrilli, George E., and Anna Marie Mueser. *Welcome Baby: A Guide to the First Six Weeks.* See Chapter 2, item 96.

338. Wheatley, Meg, and Marcie Schorr Hirsch. *Managing Your Maternity Leave.* Boston: Houghton Mifflin, 1983.

As the number of pregnant workers increases, problems about occupational health and dafety during pregnancy, as well as the issue of maternity leave are emerging. Here are helpful suggestions about state laws dealing with maternity leave, understanding legal rights, gaining the cooperation of the employer, and combining work and new parenthood.

339. Williams, Tannis, M. *Infant Care: Abstracts of the Literature.* See Chapter 9, item 451.

340. Wood, B.S. *Children and Communication: Verbal and Nonverbal Language Development.* See Chapter 5, item 236.

341. Wyckoff, Jerry, and Barbara C. Unell. *Discipline Without Shouting or Spanking.* See Chapter 3, item 166.

342. Young, Leontine. *Wednesday's Children: A Study of Child Abuse and Neglect.* New York: McGraw-Hill, 1979, reprint of 1964.

Young profiles abusing and neglectful families and the settings in which child maltreatment is most likely to occur. She discusses the response of social service agencies and the judiciary and the need for public involvement in the abuse and neglect problem.

INFANT PLAY

Deborah Lovitky Sheiman

Play. What is it? Why is it? When does it occur? From
infancy into childhood and throughout the adult years, human
beings engage in play, ranging from a simple game of peek-a-
boo to a competitive round of golf. Behavioral scientists
study how play contributes to the development of the child
and ask what improves the quality of play experiences. The
play that begins in infancy sets a foundation for a life-span
of adaptive activity.

Whether alone, or interacting with others, a child plays
because it is fun. It provides enjoyment. Babies engage in
play spontaneously, electively, and for no purpose other than
for play itself. There need be no additional motive for the
primary activity of pleasure. An atmosphere for play must
allow for the child's movement and exploration in addition to
the availability of toys and playmates.

Babies engage in three forms of play: sensory motor, symbolic, and game play. Sensory motor play is the earliest
form to emerge. Its salient feature is action or motor play.
It is evident as infants begin to manipulate and explore their
world. With the ability to reach out and grasp and to bat
one's arms and legs, infants soon learn that they can affect
their environment. Stimulation and attempts at social control
are apparent as infants discover what the person or object
will do if manipulated.

Symbolic or pretend play can develop as early as 18 months
and is normally found in most children by age 3. In order for
symbolic play to occur it is necessary that an element of
reality be transformed. Roles and objects or themes can be
altered by imagination. The young child has control over the
fantasy. The restraints of reality are lifted, leaving the
child to control the imagined act or role.

Game play is distinguished by the engagement of at least
two partners in a mutual pursuit. Each person is expected to
take turns and enact the scenario repeatedly until one party

withdraws. Game play is evident from early infancy when
parents and babies engage in interactional games such as
peek-a-boo.
    Sensory motor play, symbolic play, and game play all pro-
vide pleasurable interactions for babies. Each form has an
intrinsic quality that endures. One form is not replaced by
another as baby grows more competent. Individually, each form
becomes more structured to meet the needs of the child at each
stage of development. The infant's rolling of the ball can
turn to the preschooler's tricycling. Peek-a-boo can be replaced by board games, and an imaginary friend of three can
become the daydreaming episodes of childhood.
    Play is important in baby's growth. Maturation and ex-
perience are essential to infant's skill development. Maturation is a naturally occurring biophysical process. However,
through the medium of play, babies gain experiences. Play
allows babies to explore motor abilities, make judgments, and
test reality in a nonthreatening manner. The freedom to fail
in a play setting permits babies to test and gradually extend
their social boundaries.
    The function of play can be illustrated by the activity
of tickling baby. Tickling generally occurs in a relaxed
atmosphere where the persons are familiar, usually a parent
or caregiver. The parent feigns an assault on baby. Baby responds with laughter and gross physical movement. Underlying
this seemingly simple social interaction, the baby makes a
judgment as to whether the parent is pretending or intending
harm. If a stranger made the same assault baby would stiffen
and cry. However, through the repeated play experiences with
the trusted familiar parent, the baby has come to learn that
the attacks are pretend, a form of playing. This interaction
contributes to the infant's sense of self-esteem. Babies soon
learn that they can influence or manipulate reality. They can
prolong the tickling game by responding to the parents' pretend attacks with laughter and eye contact. Babies learn
that actions can lead to reactions by others. Behavior has
consequences. Primitive notions of participation and cooperation are conveyed as babies acquire the social rituals of
game play.
    Babies not only interact with parents, but also play with
peers and toys. They are attracted to the sensory, tactile,
and responsive properties of playthings. They enjoy toys that
predictably elicit noise or movement as a response to manipulation. The novel properties of the toy should stimulate exploration and encourage participation and/or interaction with
playmates. Before age three, realistic, structured toys are
preferable. The ability to engage in symbolic play must be
realized before the young child can mentally transform a block

into a car. With the development of imagination by around age
three, the most appealing toys become those of simple, functional design that afford children the opportunity to use
their own abilities and creative thought.

Level of development should guide the selection of infant
and toddler toys. Good play materials exercise newly developed
skills. For example, at birth to three months, babies react
to the novel visual and auditory properties of their environment. They focus on and follow moving objects and locate
sounds. Toys such as a musical rotating mobile, made of colorful plush or vinyl, build an awareness of sight and sound.

From four to eleven months babies use toys to learn about
color, texture, taste, sound and spatial relationships. Babies
are now active participants. Predictability and success in
play brings smiles of satisfaction. Favorite toys must be
in close proximity. Frustration is apparent over a dropped
or nonaccessible treasured plaything. Play gyms composed of
rattles, squeakers, spinners and bars encourage four- and
five-month-old babies to reach, handle, and grasp.

Around age five months, toys take on new perspective as
babies learn to sit. Play can now be upright or prone. Delight is evident as they practice the same skills from different posture positions. By six months, reflection of self-image
provides pleasure. Brightly colored, light-weight rattles
with mirrors mounted on the reverse side allow baby to wave
and change toy from hand to hand and see oneself in a single
experience.

Six- to eleven-month-olds enjoy music and motion. Baby
swings and bouncers provide excitement and relaxation. The
new mobility of creeping (around six months) and crawling
(around nine months) change how babies perceive and respond
to their environment. Parents can encourage the development
of mobility by placing a favorite toy just outside the reach
of baby. Carrying around, fingering, banging, and inspecting
toys bring great pleasure at this stage of development.

From 12 to 15 months, toddling mobility opens up new
avenues for exploration. Toys played with should support the
development of walking skills. Walkers with toys attached
are practical. When walking skills are refined, toddlers are
ready to include pull toys to the push-toy collection. Good
push and pull toys are used under toddler's own control and
are sound producing. Push toys allow toddlers visual validation, whereas in pull toys dragged behind the child, auditory
validation is needed to establish the toy's presence. Auditory and visual validation of toys promotes security and helps
toddlers to master the anxiety that mobility produces. Being
able to walk implies wandering farther from mother, a situation simultaneously exciting and anxiety producing.

Around 16 to 18 months, toddlers are interested in toys
that encourage motor control. Plastic beads, easy take-apart
toys, and peg boards are challenging. Toddlers are jubilant
over roughhouse play and delight in interactive games like
ball rolling. Indoor play gyms with slides, ladders, and
hiding places become enjoyable with the mastery of climbing
skills. Toys designed for self-initiated structured experiences are well used at this time. Colorful cups that nest
within one another and bright plastic rings that stack on top
of each other are popular. Affection for dolls and stuffed
animals is noticeable.

Creative activities delight 19- to 24-month-old children.
Scribbling shows some organization as toddlers gain control
over holding a crayon. Play dough invites multisensory expression of taste, touch and smell. Waterplay fascinates toddlers who are content to sit for long periods in the bathtub
filling and emptying containers of water. Additionally, tri-
cycles and other action toys promote large motor development.

There are many good toys that can be used differently and
progresively at each stage of development. These include
picture books, pots and pans, music, and sorting boxes and
blocks. For example, small blocks allow the infant an opportunity to practice grasping abilities. The toddler stacks
and tumbles them, and the preschooler uses them for construction.

Toys should never overwhelm a child. Parents are encouraged to rotate their children's playthings. Too many toys
at once can be confusing and discourage the infant or toddler
from thoroughly exploring each toy. The well-respected early
childhood educator, Dr. James Hymes, Jr., expressed the benefit
of a good toy succinctly in his statement "toys that are right
for one and two year-olds stand a chance of giving a child a
sense of power."

A note of caution is needed in regard to toys. Toys
should be large enough not to be swallowed or choked on and
safe and durable enough to withstand the inevitable sucking
and chewing and banging they will receive. Avoid glass,
splintering wood, small detachable parts, and insecurely fas-
tened joints. Manufacturers occasionally market a toy claiming
usage will benefit baby's cognitive development. Empirical
evidence generally does not support claims that cognitive
skills will appear earlier or be enhanced by the use of certain toys. Babies go through a natural sequence of cognitive
development and will use toys according to their own developmental levels.

Age ranges stated on toy packaging should also be viewed
discerningly. A frequent problem is an overly broad range
resulting in too wide an age span. A toy should challenge

and meet the developmental needs of a child, not cause frustration or boredom.

Playmates or peer relationships serve as the basic building blocks for social interaction throughout life. The toddler's comprehension of playmate's intent develops from an ability to communicate shared language. This ability to speak develops around age two. Before age two, babies relate to peers in an object-centered manner. They investigate the peer as a physical object. Attraction to the other baby's toy brings peers together. Generally, it is the toy the baby is concerned with; the peer is secondary. This can lead to parallel play where each youngster engages in mutual play without directly interacting with the other.

As toddlers approach three years, genuine social relationships become more distinguishable. Peers are interacted with as people who can initiate and respond to the actions of the playmate. As the youngster matures, the nature of peer play becomes increasingly direct and adaptive. However, it must be remembered that peer play is a social skill that will only blossom if given opportunity and practice.

Peer interaction has a positive impact on baby's development. Babies as young as 18 months can learn to manipulate a toy by copying another child. Toddlers are more likely to wander farther from their mother and try new experiences in the company of a playmate.

Peer play permits youngsters the opportunity to shift roles and experiences, thereby reducing egocentric behavior. By encountering numerous roles and emotions in play, young children learn the behaviors and emotions appropriate to their experiences. This promotes the development of a sense of empathy. Peer interaction provides the toddler with information about one part of the social world. However useful this is in fostering social development, it does not reach the magnitude of information gleaned from family and adult interactions.

Babies and young children form attachments to those they play with regularly. These affectionate bonds of infancy and toddlerhood lay the foundation for later friendships and intimate relationships. Opportunities to form these attachments are ever increasing with the popularity of cooperative child-care arrangements, such as play groups. A typical play group is composed of four or more prenursery school children who regularly meet to play under the supervision of one mother. The home where the group is held and the supervising mother charged with planning, preparing, and guiding the activities rotate with each meeting.

Play groups allow toddlers mutual involvement with play objects and direct social encounters with other children. The

secure home setting with a familiar cooperative adult helps
to stimulate early play exploration. However, the toddler is
not the only participant whose interests are served by the
play group. Mothers, particularly of first born children,
become more relaxed and confident when they view their child's
behavior repeated in other children. Observing normal toddler behavior increases mothers' competence, enjoyment, and
understanding of their own youngster.

The function and benefits of play cannot be discussed
without asking the question "What are the consequences of a
child deprived of play?" Dr. Margaret Lowenfeld in her book
Play in Childhood sums it up with:

> Play is an essential function of the passage from
> immaturity to emotional maturity. Any individual without
> the opportunities for adequate play in early life will
> go on seeking them in the stuff of adult life. Emo-
> tional satisfactions which the mind missed at the period
> to which they properly belong, do not present themselves
> later in the same form. Forces unrealized in childhood
> become an inner drive forever seeking outlet and lead
> men to express them not any longer in play (since this
> is regarded as an activity of childhood) but in competi-
> tion, anarchy and war.

BIBLIOGRAPHY

343. Aston, Athina. *Toys That Teach Your Child from Birth
      to Two*, rev. ed. William A. Emerson, ed. Charlotte,
      N.C.: East Woods Press, 1984.

      The focus is on developmental play. Ashton discusses
      all types of toys including brand-name ones and how to
      use them effectively for early stimulation. Although
      addressed to parents, the book is also helpful to teachers.

344. Attebury, Jean E., ed. *Project Plans to Build for
      Children from the Pages of Better Homes and Gardens*.
      Des Moines, Ia.: Garlinhouse, 1984.

      Instructions and diagrams are given for building over
      130 projects from toys to room design. Order forms are
      included for instructions for additional projects.

345. Beckwith, Glenwood J. *How to Make Your Backyard More Interesting Than T.V.* New York: McGraw-Hill, 1980.

Targeted to parents, the author offers helpful guidelines for creating developmentally appropriate play environments. Safety of play equipment is stressed.

346. Bell, Sally C., and Dolly Langdon. *Romper Room's Miss Sally Presents 200 Fun Things to Do with Little Kids.* Garden City, N.Y.: Doubleday, 1983.

As the title promises, this is a good book for busy parents looking for fun activities with their children.

347. Borman, Kathryn M., ed. *The Social Life of Children in a Changing Society.* Norwood, N.J.: Ablex, 1983.

This academic, multidisciplinary discussion examines childhood socialization.

348. Broad, Laura P., and Nancy T. Butterworth. *The Playgroup Handbook.* New York: St. Martin's, 1974.

The authors have prepared a useful manual for developing and managing a play group. Activities for children are listed by monthly schedules as guidelines for developmental play.

349. Bronson, Wanda. *Toddler's Behavior with Age Mates: Issues of Interaction, Cognition and Affect.* Norwood, N.J.: Ablex, 1981.

The text is based on an observational study conducted by the author. Findings should be of interest to professionals and parents who wish to understand a toddler's interaction during play.

350. Brown, Catherine Caldwell, and Allen W. Gottfried. *Play Interactions: The Role of Toys and Parental Involvement in Children's Development.* Pediatric Round Table #11, Somerville, N.J.: Johnson & Johnson, 1985.

Play Interactions explores the research findings of 20 child development authorities concerning the origin of play, play and developmental processes, the social significance of play, and consequences of play. Evidence is presented that shows play materials and parental involvement as potent factors related to the development of young children.

351. Burtt, Kent Garland. *Smart Times: A Parent's Guide to
     Quality Time with Preschoolers*. New York: Harper &
     Row, 1984.

     Parent and child interaction is reciprocal, and shared
     activities should be of interest to parents as well as
     children. The author, an authority on early education,
     presents over 200 activities that are rewarding to both.
     Although designed for children ages two, three, and four,
     many of the ideas are appropriate for even younger chil-
     dren. Written in an easy-to-follow format, free of edu-
     cational or psychological jargon, the book can be a re-
     source for professionals who work with young children,
     parents, and caregivers.

352. Castle, Kathryn. *The Infant and Toddler Handbook: In-
     vitations for Optimum Early Development*. See Chapter
     4, item 173.

353. Cherry, Clare. *Creative Play for the Developing Child*.
     Belmont, Calif.: Pitman Learning, 1976.

     The overall goals of creative play are explored along-
     side an overview of many different kinds of play activi-
     ties enjoyed by young children. Parents and profession-
     als will find this a helpful book.

354. *Consumer Guide*, Editors of. *The Complete Baby Book*.
     See Chapter 7, item 282.

355. Glazer, Tom. *Music for Ones and Twos: Songs and Games
     for the Very Young Child*. Garden City, N.Y.: Double-
     day, 1983.

     Tom Glazer, in recognition of the general and growing
     awareness of the importance of educating infants, has
     put together a collection of games and songs designed
     to delight the very youngest children. These are standard
     "classics" as well as new material.

356. Gould, Deb, et al. *Playgroups: How to Grow Your Own
     from Infancy Onward*. Cambridge, Mass.: Child Care Re-
     source Center, 1982.

     This pamphlet, which covers playgroups in the Boston
     area, presents information of value to anyone interested
     in learning how to start and run a play group.

357. Grasselli, Rose N., and Priscilla A. Hegner. *Playful
     Parenting: Games to Help Your Infants and Toddlers*

Grow Physically, Mentally and Emotionally. New York: Marek (Putnam), 1981.

The authors have designed a program to foster a child's development through play. It is built around three play groups--diaper play, toddler play, and mini play--to fit a child from six weeks to three years. There are finger play, exercise games, warm-up games, dance play, exploring activities, as well as behavioral guidelines and suggestions for other sensorimotor experiences.

358. Haas, Carolyn, et al. *Look at Me: Activities for Babies and Toddlers.* Northfield, Ill.: CBH Publishing, 1984.

Part of the Recipe for Fun Series, *Look at Me* is filled with creative activities for home and the early childhood group setting. It contains helpful ideas for parents and teachers.

359. Headley, Neith E., et al. *Play: Children's Business.* Washington, D.C.: Association for Childhood Education International, 1979.

These essays illustrate the relationship of play cognition, to development, and to socialization. Practical suggestions are offered for implementing good play experiences and selecting materials that provide children not only with opportunities for play but also comfortable challenges. There is a guide to play materials and age-appropriate toys.

360. Herron, R.E., and Brian Sutton-Smith. *Child's Play.* Melbourne, Fla.: Krieger, 1982.

The authors look at play from a scholarly point of view. Teachers and professionals in the field will find this important work most useful.

361. Honig, Alice. *Playtime Learning Games for Young Children.* See Chapter 4, item 177.

362. Johnson & Johnson Baby Products Company. *The First Wondrous Years: You and Your Baby.* See Chapter 7, item 300.

363. McCall, Robert B. *Infants: The New Knowledge.* See Chapter 4, item 183.

364. McDiarmid, N. *Loving and Learning.* See Chapter 4, item 184.

365. Marzollo, Jean. *Supertot: Creative Learning Activities
      for Children One to Three and Sympathetic Advice for
      Their Parents.* New York: Harper & Row, 1978.

      This book, a guide of how to teach your children
      while playing with them, has much helpful advice. Each
      heading is in block letters, enabling parents to flip
      through and find what is of interest to them. Marzollo
      has included lists of age-appropriate toys.

366. Marzollo, Jean, and Janice Lloyd. *Learning Through
      Play.* New York: Harper & Row, 1972.

      Organized by areas of development, rather than chrono-
      logical age, *Learning Through Play* is filled with ideas
      for play activities designed to foster learning in young
      children.

367. Mergen, B. *Play and Playthings: A Reference Guide.*
      Westport, Conn.: Greenwood, 1982.

      Mergen presents a historical reference guide to
      children's play in America. Writings on children and
      child behavior are studied in an effort to understand
      what is meant by the word "play" and what play has meant
      to children. Pictures of children playing in different
      parts of the country, in different time periods, are
      included.

368. Moore, Gary T. *Bibliography on Children and the Built
      Environment: Child Care Centers, Outdoor Play Environ-
      ments, and Other Children's Environments.* Milwaukee:
      University of Wisconsin Center for Architecture and
      Urban Planning Research, 1979.

      The bibliography was created for U.S. military in-
      stallations around the world. All of the environments
      are behaviorally based.

369. Munger, Evelyn M., and Susan J. Bowdon. *Childplay:
      Activities for Your Child's First Three Years.* New
      York: Dutton, 1983.

      The authors approach their discussion of the child
      and play from quarter years, offering the parent many
      activities and ideas for each age period.

370. Neser, Gwen, and Janna Gaughan. *Infantoddler Parenting:
      Activities for Child with Adult.* Elberon, N.J.: Uni-
      Ed Associates, 1980.

Basing their findings on a five-year research project, the authors have developed a structured program "partnership in learning," an interactive approach that provides pleasurable learning for both the infant and the adult. While all activities take place in a group setting, instructions are given for parent and child to "practice at home." Chapters include not only activities such as finger plays, puppet play, creative dramatics, but also guidelines for preparing the environment, arriving, gathering, greeting, as well as leaving and at-home follow-up.

371. Newson, John, and Elizabeth Newson. *Toys and Playthings: In Development and Remediation*. New York: Pantheon, 1979.

The authors focus on the role of toys and play in enhancing development. As a matter of fact, they feel that mother is the best toy of all. Much of the discussion is concerned with the child who is slow in making progress because of being mentally or physically handicapped. The Newsons emphasize the developmental needs of such children. Parents and teachers of all young children will benefit from this practical book.

372. Ormerod, Jan. *101 Things to Do with a Baby*. New York: Lothrop, Lee & Shepard, 1984.

Here is one of those rare books that goes directly to the core of the topic. The whole family shares in taking care of and accepting the new baby. The author presents her "thesis" via a loving six-year-old "big sister."

373. Painter, Genevieve. *Teach Your Baby*. *See* Chapter 4, item 194.

374. Pepler, D.J., and K.H. Rubin, eds. *The Play of Children*. New York: Karger, 1982.

The editors have gathered a scholarly set of contributions of interest to educators and researchers and those with a background on the literature on the topic of play. The volume is divided into five parts with two or three articles by different authors. Of special interest for the early childhood educator should be the section on "Ecological Influences on Children's Play," which highlights the impact the environment, materials, and curriculum has on young children and their development.

375. Piers, Maria W., and Genevieve M. Landau. *The Gift of*
      Play: And Why Young Children Cannot Thrive Without It.
      New York: Walker, 1980.

      Piers and Landau regard imaginative and free play as
      more valuable in a child's development than structured,
      goal-oriented programs. Play is a rehearsal for adult-
      hood and provides a transition to it. For authors, TV
      deprives a child of the imaginative and active play
      needed to make that transition. One's play affects one's
      behavior, and thus, for example, playing with guns is
      impossible to separate from violent behavior.

376. Pitcher, Evelyn G., and Lynn H. Schultz. *Boys and Girls*
      at Play: The Development of Sex Roles. New York:
      Praeger, 1983.

      This is a review of the comprehensive study of 225
      children aged two through five at play with same-sex
      or opposite-sex peers. Results from this research em-
      phasize that early social interactions form the founda-
      tion for same and opposite sex relationships in future
      years. The material can be a valuable resource for
      teachers and parents.

377. Provenzo, Eugene F., Jr., and Arlene Brett. *The Com-*
      plete Block Book. Syracuse, N.Y.: Syracuse University
      Press, 1983.

      Blocks are very important toys. They allow children
      to create and structure a world that is their own. The
      authors have chapters on the history of blocks, their
      design and use, and how they are used in contemporary
      context.

378. Robinson, Jeri. *Activities for Anyone, Anytime, Any-*
      where. Boston: Little, Brown, 1983.

      Designed for children and adults, Robinson's creative,
      imaginative book is filled with ideas for activities for
      any place and any conceivable kind of situation.

379. Rubin, Kenneth H., and Hildy S. Ross, eds. *Peer Rela-*
      tionships and Social Skills in Childhood. New York:
      Springer Verlag, 1982.

      This volume applies research to the common assumption
      that children's social skills grow and develop with age.
      Although the main concern is the emerging social rela-
      tionships among siblings, infants and toddlers, and

parents and children, the discussion is not limited to
such relationships. The text is a point of departure
for further scientific study. The book was compiled for
the academic community, but others will find it of interest too.

380. Schaefer, Charles E., and Kevin J. O'Connor. *Handbook
     of Play Therapy.* New York: Wiley, 1983.

     This textbook approaches play therapy through specific
     techniques for specific childhood disorders. It is
     directed to the practitioner and the academic community.

381. Scheffler, Hannah Nuba, ed. *Resources for Early Child-
     hood: An Annotated Bibliography and Guide for Educa-
     tors, Librarians, Health Care Professionals, and
     Parents.* See Chapter 7, item 327.

382. Schwartzman, Helen B., ed. *Play and Culture.* West
     Point, N.Y.: Leisure Press, 1980.

     Play theory, the ritual dimensions of play, linguistic
     play, children's play, recent studies of games, and
     playful and culturally relative aspects of humor are
     considered. Play has been compared and likened to
     everything, but it has rarely been viewed as a theor-
     etical resource for the study of play itself, which is
     what is examined here.

383. Sheiman, Deborah Lovitky. "A Comparison of Raters' and
     Manufacturers' Opinions of Appropriate Ages and Skills
     Needed to Use Selected Toys." Ann Arbor: Disserta-
     tion Abstracts International, 1977 (unpublished dis-
     sertation--Temple University).

     This observational survey of common infant and toddler
     toys focuses on blocks, play gyms, push toys, rattles,
     and mobiles. The author discusses the skills necessary
     for each toy to be beneficial to a child. Inherent in
     this dissertation is the assumption that good toys help a
     child to initiate experiences facilitated by the design
     of a toy.

384. Singer, Dorothy, and Jerome Singer. *Partners in Play:
     A Step-by-Step Guide to Imaginative Play in Children.*
     New York: Harper & Row, 1977.

     The authors feel fantasy and creativity can be stimu-
     lated with a minimum of props. Both make believe and
     pretending process complex information, help develop

self-awareness, develop flexibility in new social situations, foster verbal skills, and develop emotional awareness in children.

385. Singer, Jerome. *The Child's World of Make-Believe: Experimental Studies of Imaginative Play.* New York: Academic Press, 1973.

    Singer's thoughtful study of fantasy and its implications is recommended for teachers of young children. It is very readable.

386. Smith, Susan, and Melinda King. *Happy Birthday: A Guide to Special Parties for Children.* Lake Oswego, Ore.: White Pine Press, 1983.

    Here is a party book with a difference. It concentrates on the homemade and inexpensive.

387. Sparling, Joseph, and Isabelle Lewis. *Learning Games for the First Three Years: A Guide to Parent-Child Play.* New York: Walker, 1983.

    A parent can select from 100 games to play with the under-three-year-old child. Their goals range from social and emotional development to intellectual and creative development.

388. Sponseller, Doris, ed. *Play as a Learning Medium.* Washington, D.C.: National Association for the Education of Young Children, 1974.

    The contributors, all outstanding educators, focus primarily on the cognitive developmental role of play. Throughout the articles emphasize that play has a role in a child's total development.

389. Strom, Robert D. *Growing Through Play: Readings for Parents and Teachers.* Monterey, Calif.: Wadsworth, 1981.

    This is a great book as a reference in the home. There is one full section on play for parent and child development.

390. Weininger, Otto. *Play and Education: The Basic Tool for Early Childhood Learning.* Springfield, Ill.: Thomas, 1979.

    Adults often assume that the child who is playing is not really doing anything of value. This text highlights the fact, backed by research, that through play a child recreates the world and learns to understand it. Weininger helps parents and teachers increase their effectiveness as educators.

391. Winn, Marie, and Mary Ann Porcher. *The Playgroup Book.* New York: Penguin, 1972.

The authors, both pioneers in early education, wrote their book to encourage and assist parents in organizing and running a successful play group. While they are concerned with three- and four-year-olds, the suggestions given apply for any age group.

INFANT EDUCATION

Kathleen Pullan Watkins

Many of the very earliest educational philosophers recognized the importance of the infant's mother as first teacher
and primary influence on early growth and development. For
centuries, even in the absence of a baby's parents, an extended family of siblings, grandparents, and other relatives
supplied the support and experiences that facilitated early
learning. However, changes in family structure, lifestyle,
work situations, and new knowledge about child development
have strongly influenced the persons involved and the milieu
in which early child rearing takes place.

At the conclusion of World War II, many of the women who
had replaced service men in the work force continued to be
employed outside the home. Contributing to this change in the
roles of women was an increase in the number of single-parent
families and the civil rights and women's movements, the latter
two of which stressed the need to strive for personal freedom
and fulfillment of individual potential.

From the outset, child care was seen as a necessary evil,
designed to replace the family only when no other options were
available and women were forced to work outside the home by
unfortunate family circumstances. The programs that existed
were designed for children in the three- to five-year age
range, and little was available for infants and toddlers.
It has only been within the past 25 years that major changes
have occurred in attitudes toward and options for infant care
and education. Underlying these changes are several influential factors, including the growth of the early childhood profession and extensive research into the value of learning in
infancy. Until the 1960s, learning research was focused primarily upon the school-age child, as the infant was seen as
incapable of active learning and as a poor subject for empirical study.

As the importance of the first five years of life became
apparent, and those working with young children began merging

into professional groups, these individuals and the public-at-large began to take a second look at what might appropriately constitute early care and experience. At first, day care and early childhood education were viewed distinctly, the former being devoted to custodial care of the child. Recently, however, the vast majority of programs are aimed at the needs of the whole child--physical, cognitive, and social-emotional. Today, even the six-week-old participating in a quality child development program is provided with the setting, materials, experiences, and adult involvement designed to promote maximum individual development.

Infant care and education must be intertwined for a very simple reason. Unable to create their own learning experience, infants rely upon the important adults in their lives to create learning for them. Therefore, the caregiving routines that comprise a baby's day, such as feeding, diapering, play-times, and interactions with others, become educational experiences. When adults talk to infants, language development is facilitated. Playing simple games and mouthing and handling objects provided by caregivers promotes the growth of those cognitive skills essential for all human learning, while adult-child interactions form the basis for interpersonal relationships throughout life. There are, in fact, no aspects of child development that do not have their roots in the experiences of infancy. It is for these reasons that a parent's choice of child care/early learning situations may be crucial to a baby's well-being.

The types of infant care and learning programs available for children in the birth to three-year age range are many and varied. In fact, many parents become confused when attempting to identify a child-care situation that best meets the family's unique needs. Family day care, for example, provides programs for small groups of children in private homes. State licensing or registration is generally needed to legally operate a family day-care home, although no early childhood certification or previous experience is required for home managers. As they are situated in private residences, day-care homes are often conveniently located near the families requiring services. Many parents prefer this type of program for the home-style setting and the intimacy possible in infant-caregiver relationships due to the small number of children enrolled (usually no more than six). In the 1980s, family day care is the most widely used type of child-care situation.

The second largest type of infant program is the infant-care center. While some programs are federally funded, the vast majority of centers are operated by churches, by community groups, or as businesses. Center-based care provides a daily program for 35 to 50 children, although the capacity

of some programs may be smaller or larger. Children may be
divided into multiage groups or may be separated according to
age, a common practice when infants and toddlers are in care.
The extended-day hours (usually from 7:00 A.M. until 6:00 P.M.),
the small adult-child ratio required by day-care regulations,
and a trained and experienced staff are only some of the reasons that many parents feel that center-based infant care best
meets their needs.

The community or privately operated nursery is another
style of infant-care program. Unlike day-care centers, nursery school programs are usually open part-day. That is,
children attend for periods from two to six hours. Reasons
for enrolling a child in a nursery school program may go beyond a parent's need for a part-time day-care situation.
With the trend toward smaller families, many desire that their
children have the early social experiences with peers that
they would otherwise enjoy with siblings. These same parents
often find invaluable the support provided by a network of
families with young children.

One of the first of the modern forms of infant education,
also designed to provide parent support, is the neighborhood
play group. From one to three times weekly, meeting in one
another's homes, mothers and their infants gather to allow
baby play time, share child-rearing and family problems, and
have refreshment. Not unlike the quilting bee of pioneer
days, the play group lacks only the input of more experienced
grandparents. Children benefit from their interactions with
other babies and the advice and information exchanged by their
mothers.

Of the types of infant programs discussed thus far, one
of the newest is employer-sponsored child care. Designed as
an employee benefit, or aimed at improving attendance and the
quality of work by eliminating fears related to child care,
the advantages to the family are many. Parents and infants
need not be separated by distance during the day, and when
work schedules permit, many centers encourage parents to participate in classroom activities with their babies. If a
child becomes ill during the day, parents are nearby to assume
necessary care. Although limited in number at present, employer-sponsored child care may well be the wave of the future,
as both family and business profit from it.

Borrowed from time-honored British tradition is what may
be the ultimate in individualized infant care and education,
the nanny. There are now at least four American training
programs through which individuals are prepared to work exclusively for one family, in full charge of its children.
Such infant-care arrangements are considered ideal by parents
who desire year-round, full-day care for the infant provided
in their own home.

Given the broad range of available services, what resources
exist to assist parents and those who refer families to child
care? How does a parent or other interested party recognize
a quality infant program? These are two commonly asked questions for which there are answers.

Quality programs do exist, and there are many public and
private agencies that assist persons looking for child-care
services. For example, state agencies that license child-care
facilities (usually a bureau of children's programs or office
of day-care services) provide at no charge lists of child
development programs and checklists consumers may use to help
identify quality services. The federal government, along with
major early childhood education organizations, provides
similar information in the form of booklets and pamphlets.
There are a growing number of consulting firms devoted exclusively to helping parents identify the program or school
best suited to child and family needs. These can be found
listed under "educational consultants" in the telephone directory.

Local colleges and universities with departments of early
childhood education, child care, or child development are yet
another source of information about programs for infants.
Parents or community members may contact infant specialists,
many of whom supervise student teachers and, therefore, have
an intimate knowledge of area child development centers.

Parents who are seeking specialized programs for an exceptional infant should consult with their child's pediatrician.
However, many of the organizations that represent the needs
of handicapped persons, such as the Association for Retarded
Citizens or the Council for Exceptional Children, may also
provide valuable assistance.

The characteristics of a good infant program are neither
complex nor difficult for the untrained eye to distinguish.
They can be observed by any interested individual willing to
spend a morning visiting an early childhood center. These
features may be described as follows:

The center or home should have posted the appropriate
licenses required by the city and state in which it is
located. Such written approval automatically tells a great
deal about certain safety and health-related features and
qualifications of staff (in centers only), as the regulations
for child-care facilities are fairly strict. A prospective
consumer should obtain a copy of current guidelines for infant
programs and should expect ready answers to questions about
personnel employed, curriculum and daily schedule, nutrition,
and other features. Additional information about the program
is available through parents who have used the program's

services in the past or who currently have children enrolled.
A high-quality infant center should be pleased to provide in-
quiring parties with the names of families who are willing to
act as program references.

An infant program should employ experienced, nurturing
caregivers. Most states require that degreed, certified
teachers act as group supervisors in child-care centers.
However, possession of a university diploma does not guarantee
that an individual is endowed with the skills and personal
qualities essential in infant caregivers. Many family day-
care managers and others employed in child care lack college
degrees but are rich in knowledge and concern for the needs
of children. Such persons tend to exude warmth and a loving
attitude, and the children around them reflect the excellence
of care received through manner and behavior. Simply put,
when the program is of high quality and the caregiving appropriate, children appear bright-eyed, happy, and at ease in their
surroundings. They babble and talk, move about freely, and
eagerly explore the environment. These babies openly welcome
the interactions and touch of their surrogate parents.

There is a positive and growing trend in infant-care
centers toward the permanent assignment of one or two adults
to the care of each infant. These adults are called "primary
caregivers." The purpose of the roles of these personnel is
to foster attachment to subsidiary adult figures, as well as
to cut down on the spread of germs and illness, a serious
concern in day-care facilities.

The daily program of a quality infant program should be
varied and aimed at facilitating overall child development:
physical, cognitive, and social-emotional. Toys should be
available that may be grasped and mouthed without danger to
the baby, as this is one of the ways in which much early
learning takes place. The environment should be spotlessly
clean, well lit, and provide spaces for infants to lie on the
floor, crawl, or toddle. Parents should be leery of any center or home in which infants are consistently confined to
cribs, playpens, walkers, or highchairs. Motor development
is most likely to proceed normally if children are free to
move about. Bright colors, people and animal pictures and
mirrors at eye level, infant books, and sensory development
toys are other examples of excellent equipment for infant education. It should be noted that the newest and most expensive
equipment and most beautifully appointed facility are not, by
themselves, indicators of program excellence. Much depends upon
the quality of adult-baby interaction. It is when caregivers
become guides or facilitators of infant play, rather than
mere observers or controllers of it, that babies are able to
make the very most of their environment.

A caution is inserted here with regard to the trend toward developing genius in infancy. Proponents of the "superbaby syndrome," as it is sometimes called, state that daily lessons in mathematics, reading, music, and other subjects taught by parents and infant educators will result in measurable increases in a baby's IQ during the early years. However, many of the most respected specialists in infant development and learning, such as Burton White and T. Berry Brazelton, suggest that applying pressure to learn during the very early years of life can result in damage to self-esteem and fear of learning situations, if a youngster feels unable to meet parental expectations. Infant development expert Magda Gerber states, "Infants do what they can do and should not be expected to do what they cannot do."

One of the problems frequently associated with leaving an infant in the care of another are the feelings of worry experienced by the child's parents. These emotions are both real and genuinely troubling and while they persist can interfere with an adult's work, family relationships, and even sleeping and eating habits. Examples of parental concerns include:

> "What if my baby becomes ill or is injured, and I am not there?"

> "How can a stranger give my baby the sort of love that I do at home?"

> "Will my baby forget me and learn to love the caregiver instead?"

> "I will miss all of the important firsts in my baby's life. He will say his first words and take his first steps without me!"

None of these fears should be shrugged off as insignificant or unimportant, for parents' comfort with their infant-care program is essential. A good caregiver is not insensitive to family needs and will attempt to address these along with those of the infant. By sharing a baby's "firsts," encouraging parents to be part of the program, and acknowledging the importance of a mother and father's roles in the life of the child, the care provider can do much to alleviate parental apprehension. In this way, caregivers become trusted family friends and partners with parents in the effort to create a happy, secure, and loving world for their infant.

A prominent Philadelphia attorney, who is also a busy wife and mother, says proudly of the family that cares for her infant son,

> They treat him as if he were their own child. They

worry when he does not feel well, and are proud when
he learns something new. It is as if he had another
set of loving grandparents, an extended family.

BIBLIOGRAPHY

392. Adler, Sol, et al., eds. *Lesson Plans for the Infant
      and Toddler. A Sequential Oral Communications Pro-
      gram for Clinicians and Teachers.* See Chapter 4,
      item 167.

393. Ainsworth, Mary D., M.C. Blehar, E. Waters, and S. Wall.
      *Patterns of Attachment: A Psychological Study of the
      Strange Situation.* See Chapter 3, item 99.

394. Alvino, Jamas, and *Gifted Children's Newsletter* Staff.
      *Parents' Guide to Raising a Gifted Child: Recognizing
      and Developing Your Child's Potential.* See Chapter
      6, item 237.

395. Anistasiow, Nicholas J., and Michael L. Hanes. *Lan-
      guage Patterns of Poverty Children.* See Chapter 5,
      item 209.

396. Aston, Athina. *Toys That Teach Your Child from Birth
      to Two.* See Chapter 8, item 343.

397. Auerbach, Stevanne. *Choosing Child Care: A Guide for
      Parents.* New York: Dutton, 1981.

      Today many families face the question of choosing
      quality child care. Here, the author offers practical,
      step-by-step advice on how to find the right arrangements,
      including checklists to use in evaluating each type of
      child care suggested, helpful information on how to
      budget child-care costs and what questions to ask of
      prospective caretakers, baby-sitters, and directors of
      day-care centers.

398. Bailey, Rebecca Anne, and Elsie Carter Burton. *The
      Dynamic Self: Activities to Enhance Infant Develop-
      ment.* See Chapter 4, item 168.

399. Belsky, Jay, et al. *The Child in the Family.* *See* Chapter 3, item 101.

400. Biber, Barbara. *Early Education and Psychological Development.* *See* Chapter 3, item 102.

401. Broad, Laura P., and Nancy T. Butterworth. *The Playgroup Handbook.* *See* Chapter 8, item 348.

402. Bronson, Wanda. *Toddler's Behavior with Age Mates: Issues of Interaction, Cognition and Affect.* *See* Chapter 8, item 350.

403. Brunner, Jerome. *Human Growth and Development.* *See* Chapter 4, item 171.

404. Burtt, Kent Garland. *Smart Times: A Parent's Guide to Quality Time with Preschoolers.* *See* Chapter 8, item 351.

405. Caldwell, Bettye M., and Donald J. Stedman, eds. *Infant Education: A Guide for Helping Handicapped Children in the First Three Years.* *See* Chapter 6, item 238.

406. Cass-Beggs, Barbara. *Your Baby Needs Music.* *See* Chapter 4, item 172.

407. Castle, Kathryn. *The Infant and Toddler Handbook: Invitations for Optimum Early Development.* *See* Chapter 4, item 173.

408. Catoldo, Christine Z. *Infant and Toddler Programs: A Guide to Very Early Childhood Education.* Reading, Mass.: Addison-Wesley, 1983.

409. Clarke-Stewart, Alison. *Daycare.* Cambridge, Mass.: Harvard University Press, 1982.

      The author provides a relevant overview of day care, including a brief history, current status, aspects of programs most likely to promote child growth and development, qualities and styles for effective caregiving, and a description of day-care alternatives.

410. Coleen, C., F. Glantz, and D. Calore. *Day Care Centers in the U.S.* Cambridge, Mass.: ABJ Associates, 1979.

      A compilation of results from the National Day Care Study, this report provides a thorough analysis of the characteristics of the consumers, staff, facilities, finances, and regulations pertaining to day-care centers.

411. Connor, Frances P., G. Gordon Williamson, and John M. Siepp. *Program Guide for Infants and Toddlers with Neuromotor and Other Developmental Disabilities.* See Chapter 6, item 240.

412. Cruttenden, Alan. *Language in Infancy and Childhood: A Linguistic Introduction to Language Acquisition.* See Chapter 5, item 215.

413. Davis, W.F. *Educator's Resource Guide to Special Education.* See Chapter 6, item 242.

414. DeVilliers, Peter A., and Jill G. DeVilliers. *Early Language.* See Chapter 5, item 218.

415. Dittman, L., ed. *The Infants We Care For.* Washington, D.C.: National Association for the Education of Young Children, 1973.

    A series of essays presents aspects of infant programming by child-care specialists. Staff selection and training and program evaluation chapters are provided with outlines for staff in-service sessions and suggestions for assessing program effectiveness.

416. Durrell, Doris. *The Critical Years: A Guide for Dedicated Parents.* See Chapter 3, item 113.

417. Evans, J. *Working with Parents of Handicapped Children.* Reston, Va.: Council for Exceptional Children, 1980.

    This volume will aid the early childhood education teacher in understanding and responding appropriately to the feelings and needs of the parents of handicapped children. It provides ways for teachers to examine their own feelings about parents and youngsters and offers guidelines for meeting and talking with families.

418. Genishi, Celia, and Ann Dyson. *Language Assessment in the Early Years.* See Chapter 5, item 220.

419. Glazer, Tom. *Music for Ones and Two: Songs and Games for the Very Young Child.* See Chapter 8, item 355.

420. Gonzalez-Mena, Janet, and Dianne Widmeyer Eyer. *In-fancy and Caregiving.* Palo Alto, Calif.: Mayfield, 1980.

Meshing theory with practical application, this book will guide those involved--parents and professionals--in the care of infants. Included is an infant-care curriculum, one that emphasizes the promotion of the infant's total development.

421. Haas, Carolyn, et al. *Look at Me: Activities for Babies and Toddlers.* See Chapter 8, item 358.

422. Herron, R.E., and Brian Sutton-Smith. *Child's Play.* See Chapter 8, item 360.

423. Honig, Alice S. *Playtime Learning Games for Young Children.* See Chapter 4, item 177.

424. Honig, Alice S., and J. Ronald Lally. *Infant Caregiving: A Design for Training.* Syracuse, N.Y.: Syracuse University Press, 1981.

Specifically designed for trainers of infant care-givers, this handbook is clear and direct in giving guidelines and instructions. Features are caregiver behavior assessment checklists, a Piaget task checklist, material on abused infants and infant sexuality, as well as special training topics dealing with handicapping conditions and special needs.

425. Hopper, Robert, and Rita J. Naremore. *Children's Speech.* See Chapter 5, item 221.

426. Kagan, Jerome, Richard B. Kearsley, and Philip R. Zelazo. *Infancy: Its Place in Human Development.* See Chapter 3, item 123.

427. Kaye, Peggy. *Games for Reading: Playful Ways to Help Your Child Read.* See Chapter 10, item 462.

428. Lee, D.M. *Children and Language: Reading and Writing, Talking and Listening.* See Chapter 5, item 224.

429. Lehane, Stephen. *Help Your Baby Learn: 100 Piaget-Based Activities for the First Two Years of Life.* See Chapter 4, item 181.

430. Lichtenstein, Robert, and Harry Ireton. *Preschool Screening: Identifying Young Children with Develop-*

mental and Educational Problems. See Chapter 6, item
249.

431. McDiarmid, N. *Loving and Learning.* See Chapter 4,
item 184.

432. McMurphy, J.R. *The Daycare and Preschool Handbook for
Churches.* Chappaqua, N.Y.: Christian Herald Books,
1981.

McMurphy's book is designed to furnish step-by-step
guidelines for those developing a church-sponsored day-
care or preschool program. All aspects of planning and
implementing a program are covered with special emphasis
on the relationship between the program and the church.

433. Maxim, George W. *The Sourcebook: Activities to Enrich
Programs for Infants and Young Children.* See Chapter
4, item 188.

434. Maxim, G.W. *The Very Young: Guiding Children from Infancy Through the Early Years.* See Chapter 4, item
189.

435. Nelson, Keith, ed. *Children's Language,* vols. 1–4.
See Chapter 5, item 229.

436. Painter, Genevieve. *Teach Your Baby.* See Chapter 4,
item 194.

437. Pitcher, Evelyn G., and Lynn H. Schultz. *Boys and
Girls at Play: The Development of Sex Roles.* See
Chapter 8, item 376.

438. Pushaw, David R. *Teach Your Child to Talk: A Parent
Guide.* See Chapter 5, item 232.

439. Ramey, C.T., and P.L. Trohanis, eds. *Finding and Educating High-Risk Handicapped Infants.* See Chapter 6,
item 255.

440. Safford, Phillip L. *Teaching Young Children with
Special Needs.* See Chapter 6, item 25.

441. Sattler, J.M. *Assessment of Children's Intelligence
and Special Abilities,* 2nd ed. See Chapter 4, item
198.

442. Scheffler, Hannah Nuba, ed. *Resources for Early Child-hood: An Annotated Bibliography and Guide for Educa-tors, Librarians, Health Care Professionals, and Parents. See* Chapter 7, item 327.

443. Sheiman, D. *A Comparison of Raters' and Manufacturers' Opinions of Appropriate Ages and Skills Needed to Use Selected Toys. See* Chapter 8, item 383.

444. Siegel-Gorelick, Bryna. *The Working Parent's Guide to Child Care: How to Find the Best Care for Your Child.* Boston: Little, Brown, 1983.

     This is a useful book for parents who are considering possible day-care arrangements for their child. The author outlines, step-by-step, what types of day-care facilities there are, what services one can expect, how much it will cost, how to recognize quality day care, how to help the child adjust, and how to handle difficulties that may arise.

445. Singer, Jerome. *The Child's World of Make-Believe: Experimental Studies of Imaginative Play. See* Chapter 8, item 385.

446. Strom, Robert D. *Growing Through Play: Readings for Parents and Teachers. See* Chapter 8, item 389.

447. Taylor, Denny. *Family Literacy. Young Children Learn-ing to Read and Write. See* Chapter 10, item 466.

448. Weber, Evelyn. *Ideas Influencing Early Childhood Educa-tion: A Theoretical Analysis.* New York: Teachers College, Columbia University, 1984.

     In a readable style, the author traces the roots of ideas that have stimulated the thinking of generations of early childhood educators. Contributions by seminal philosophers and psychologists from Plato to Piaget are presented, developing a cumulative perspective that lends itself toward the understanding of early childhood education as it exists today. Weber has written a rele-vant book for students, educators, policymakers, and teachers.

449. Weininger, Otto. *Play and Education: The Basic Tool for Early Childhood Learning. See* Chapter 8, item 390.

450. Weissbourd, Bernice, and Judith S. Musick, eds. *Infants: Their Social Environments.* See Chapter 3, item 164.

451. Williams, Tannis M. *Infant Care: Abstracts of the Literature.* Washington, D.C.: Child Welfare League of America, 1972.

     A major area of concern to professionals working with school-age parents is finding the best way to help them meet the needs of their infants. This work represents an extensive review of the literature in order to learn as much as possible about the needs of young parents and their infants. Priority was given to materials that addressed questions concerning infant development, infant care, infant education and intervention, day care, mother-infant interaction, child-rearing practices, and teenage parenting.

452. Wood, B.S. *Children and Communication: Verbal and Nonverbal Language Development.* See Chapter 5, item 236.

BOOKS AND BABIES

Hannah Nuba-Scheffler

> You may have tangible wealth untold:
> Caskets of jewels and coffers of gold,
> Richer than I you can never be -
> I had a Mother who read to me.
>
> "The Reading Mother," *Best Loved
> Poems of the American People*.
> Strickland Gillilan

One of the most satisfying forms of verbal communication between child and adult is that magical moment of "being read to." "Read me a story" is the preschooler's frequent refrain, and even the youngest toddler will manage self and book into the cozy lap of a willing adult.

Although bedtime stories and storytelling have always been a universal tradition, adults rarely realize the profound impact this interaction has on the child's total development, especially in the area of communication skills. In fact, reading a story to a child is one of the most valuable and satisfying activities a child and adult can share. For the child, being read to in a warm and loving setting is a deeply fulfilling experience, bringing about a feeling of trust and security that spans a lifetime.

Indeed, in such an atmosphere, the seeds for early literacy and love for literature are planted.

As part of my work in The New York Public Library Early Childhood Resource and Information Center, I am often asked by expectant or new parents about the best time for introducing books to young children. My answer is always: "Right now."

I suggest that when considering the newborn's furniture needs, a bookshelf, no matter how simple, be included. As "starter" books, there should be some sturdy, colorful board books awaiting the baby's arrival home from the hospital. Included should also be some "best-loved" classics for (to quote Professor Bernice Cullinan) "handing down the magic."

I also suggest that parents play the "conversation game" with baby from day one. Gentle, relaxed conversation (albeit one-sided at first) provides a rich learning environment for the infant from the beginning, while tending to have a soothing effect on the interacting parent as well.

This is also the ideal time for acquainting baby with nursery rhymes, poetry, songs, and stories.

If reading to infants right from the start were only done for the sheer pleasure-giving, pleasure-receiving experience of it all, it would still be a most valuable interaction between parent and child. Research, however, shows that the benefits of this activity soar beyond the immediately observable results.

Findings indicate that early exposure to books leads very early on to the infant's use of books in "reading-like ways," as Don Holdaway expresses it in *The Foundations of Literacy*. This "play-reading," along with "pretend-reading," "learned-by-heart reading," and other "reading-like-behavior" signals a giant step toward later, independent reading. As a special bonus, alongside this "emergent reading," there is (in Holdaway's words) "an equally spontaneous involvement in writing-like behavior."

Dorothy Butler, in her book, *Babies Need Books*, firmly states that there is nothing "magic" going on in the way early experiences with books produce early, eager readers. "A baby is learning about the way language arises from the page each time a parent opens a book."

Bernice Cullinan, in her essay in *Resources for Early Childhood*, stresses the connection between reading and pleasure and the wealth of wonderful literature available for sharing with children. "When daily reading-aloud sessions become a time for pleasure, children build a love of story from their earliest days."

Children's librarians have long believed in the value of reading to children. Distinguished librarian and storyteller Naomi Noyes (in *Resources for Childhood*) shares the thought that "reading aloud is a real pleasure throughout life since it fosters intimacy and sharing in addition to giving added dimension to the printed page."

Under the direction of Barbara Rollock, noted librarian, educator, and Coordinator of Children's Services, The New York Public Library, infant and toddler programs are offered in many children's libraries, with finger games and simple crafts added to the reading of age-appropriate books. Due to Mrs. Rollock's innovative leadership, a new dimension has been added to library service through the establishment of The New York Public Library Early Childhood Resource and Information Center in New York City's Greenwich Village. In

addition to offering an extensive collection of books (for
borrowing) on child development, early education, and special
needs, there are books and puzzles to borrow for children.
Focus is on materials that promote the child's development in
a variety of ways, especially in language development and pre-
literacy skills.

The Center's Family Room provides a child-centered, developmental environment that fosters the concept of the
parent as the child's first teacher and encourages the interaction between parent and child. It has a block area, house-
keeping and play space, picture-book nook, as well as rocking
horses, rocking chairs, sliding gym, playpens, and infant/
toddler learning tools. Leading educators offer workshops
and seminars that cover a wide variety of topics related to
childhood. For infants and toddlers, "Toddler-Story" programs
are presented regularly.

While lap stories are best for infants, the age of two
is ideal for introducing books to children in a library group
setting. By age two, children have developed a strong command
of language. They love picture books about familiar experiences, with lilting repetitions and colorful, recognizable
illustrations.

Two-year-olds are very concrete in their thinking and not
ready to deal with subtle plot lines, abstractions, or fine
distinctions. Book experiences for the toddler have until
now been mainly on the lap of a caring adult. In the library
setting, children still need to see the book close up, page
by page, with the librarian occasionally tracing a finger
under the text (as parents should do at home) to show the
letter-sound-meaning connection.

As the children take their cues from the sounds, the
printed symbols on the page, the meaning and enjoyment of the
story, the illustrations, and repeated listening experiences,
a lifelong link between reading and delight will have been
forged.

Books for Babies: A Sampler

Ahlberg, Janet. *The Baby's Catalogue*. Boston: Little Brown,
1983.

Alexander, Anne. *ABC of Cars and Trucks*. New York: Doubleday,
1971.

Aliki. *Hush Little Baby*. Spokane: Treehouse, 1968.

Bang, Molly. *Ten, Nine, Eight*. New York: Greenwillow, 1983.

Battaglia, Aurelis. *Animal Sounds*. New York: Western, 1981.

Bayley, Nicola. *Elephant Cat*. New York: Knopf, 1984.
(Other titles in this series: *Parrot Cat*, *Crab Cat*, *Spider Cat*, *Polar Bear Cat*.)

Brown, Margaret. *Goodnight Moon*. New York: Harper & Row, 1947.

Bruna, Dick. *Miffy*. Los Angeles: Price, Stern, Sloan, 1984.
(Other titles available in this series.)

Burningham, John. *The Baby*. New York: Harper & Row, 1975.
(Other titles available in this series.)

——. *Mr. Gumpy's Motorcar*. New York: Harper & Row, 1976.

——. *Mr. Gumpy's Outing*. New York: Harper & Row, 1971.

——. *Number Play Series*. New York: Harper & Row, 1971.
(Titles available in this series: *Pigs Plus*, *Ride Off*, *Read One*, *Five Down*, *Count Up*, *Just Cats*.)

Campbell, Rod. *Dear Zoo*. New York: Scholastic Inc., 1983.

Carle, Eric. *The Very Hungry Caterpillar*. New York: Putnam, 1969.

Cartwright, Stephen. *Find the Piglet*. Tulsa: EDC Publications, 1984.
(Similar titles in this series: *Find the Teddy*, *Find the Puppy*, *Find the Bird*, *Find the Duck*, *Find the Kitten*.)

Chandoha, Walter. *Puppies and Kittens*. New York: Platt & Munk, 1983.
(Other titles available in the Teddy Board books series.)

Chorao, Kay. *The Baby's Bedtime Book*. New York: Dutton, 1984.

Crews, Donald. *Freight Train*. New York: Greenwillow, 1978.

Dunn, Phoebe. *Farm Animals*. New York: Random House, 1984.

Emberly, Ed. *One Wide River to Cross*. Englewood Cliffs, N.J.: Prentice-Hall, 1966.

Ets, Marie. *Play with Me*. New York: Viking, 1955.

Feelings, Muriel. *Jambo Means Hello*. New York: Dial, 1974.

Ford, George. *Baby's First Picture Book*. New York: Random House, 1969.

Freschet, Bernice. *Where's Henrietta Hen?* New York: Putnam, 1980.

Gag, Wanda. *ABC Bunny*. New York: Coward, McCann & Geoghegan, 1933.

Gerstein, Mordecai. *Follow Me*. New York: Morrow, 1983.

Ginsburg, Mirra. *Chick and the Duckling*. New York: Macmillan, 1972.

———. *Good Morning Chick*. New York: Greenwillow, 1980.

Greene, Carol. *Shine, Sun*. Chicago: Children's Press, 1983.

Harvey, Paul. *Turtle*. New York: Little Simon/Simon & Schuster, 1984.

Hawkins, Colin. *Adding Animals*. New York: Putnam, 1983.

———. *What Time Is It, Mr. Wolf?* New York: Putnam, 1983.
(Other titles in this series: *Seahorse*, *Starfish*, *Sunfish*.)

Hill, Eric. *At Home*. New York: Random House, 1983.
(Other titles in this series: *My Pets*, *The Park*, *Up There*.)

———. *Spot Goes to the Beach*. New York: Putnam, 1985.
(Other titles in this series: *Where's Spot?*, *Spot's First Christmas*, *Spot's Birthday Party*, *Spot Goes to School*, *Spot's First Walk*. Some of these books are also available in Spanish.)

Hoban, Tana. *What Is It?* New York: Greenwillow, 1985.

———. *1, 2, 3*. New York: Greenwillow, 1985.

Hutchins, Pat. *Good Night Owl*. New York: Macmillan, 1972.

———. *Rosie's Walk*. New York: Macmillan, 1968.

———. *Titch*. New York: Macmillan, 1971.

Kalan, Robert. *Jump Frog, Jump!* New York: Greenwillow, 1981.

Keats, Ezra Jack. *Over in the Meadow*. Phoenix: Four Winds Press, 1971.

———. *Snowy Day*. New York: Viking, 1962.

———. *Whistle for Willie*. New York: Viking, 1964.

Krasilovsky, Phyllis. *The Very Little Boy*. New York: Doubleday, 1962.

———. *The Very Little Girl*. New York: Doubleday, 1953.

Krauss, Ruth. *The Carrot Seed*. New York: Harper & Row, 1945.

Kunhardt, Dorothy. *Pat the Bunny*. New York: Golden Books, 1942.

———. *Pat the Cat*. New York: Golden Books, 1984.

Lilly, Kenneth. *Animals in the Country.* New York: Little
Simon/Simon & Schuster, 1982.
(Other titles in this series: *Animals of the Ocean, Ani-
mals at the Zoo, Animals in the Jungle, Animals on the
Farm.*)

Lionni, Leo. *Where?* New York: Pantheon, 1983.
(Other titles in this series: *When?, What?, Who?*)

Luton, Michele. *Little Chick's Mother and All the Others.*
New York: Viking, 1983.

McCue, Lisa. *Corduroy's Day.* New York: Viking, 1985.
(Other titles in this series: *Corduroy's Party, Corduroy's
Toys.*)

McNaught, Harry. *Words to Grow On.* New York: Random House,
1984.

Mother Goose Board Books. *Lullabies.* New York: Little Simon/
Simon & Schuster, 1984.
(Other titles in this series: *ABC Rhymes, Kitten Rhymes,
Counting Rhymes.*)

Munari, Bruno. *Jimmy Has Lost His Cap: Where Can It Be?*
New York: Collins, 1959.

Muntean, Michaela. *Alligator's Garden.* New York: Dial, 1984.

Nakatani, Chiyoko. *My Day on the Farm.* New York: Crowell,
1975.

Nister, Ernest. *The Great Panorama Picture Book.* New York:
Delacorte, 1982. (Originally published in 1895.)

———. *Merry Go Round.* New York: Philomel, 1983.
(Originally published in 1897.)

Ormerod, Jan. *Messy Baby.* New York: Lothrop, 1985.
(Similar titles in this series: *Dad's Back, Reading,
Sleeping.*)

Oxenbury, Helen. *Dressing.* New York: Little Simon/Simon &
Schuster, 1981.
(Other titles in this series: *Playing, Working, Family,
Friends.*)

Parish, Peggy. *I Can--Can You?* New York: Greenwillow, 1980.
(Other titles available in this series.)

Parsons, Virginia. *First Things* (a Golden Block book). New
York: Western, 1982.

Peter Rabbit's Pockets. New York: Little Simon/Simon &
Schuster, 1982.
(Other titles in this series: *Baby's Pockets, The Velveteen
Rabbit's Pockets, Teddy Bear's Pockets.*)

Petersham, Maud. *The Box with Red Wheels*. New York: Collier, 1973.

———. *The Circus Baby*. New York: Macmillan, 1968.

Pienkowski, Jan. *Gossip*. New York: Greenwillow, 1980.
(Other titles available in this series.)

Prelutsky, Jack. *It's Snowing, It's Snowing*. New York: Greenwillow, 1984.

Real Mother Goose Husky Books. New York: Rand McNally, 1983.

Rockwell, Anne. *My Dentist*. New York: Greenwillow, 1975.
(Other available titles: *My Doctor*, *Supermarket*, *Toolbox*.)

Rubel, Nicole. *Me and My Kitty*. New York: Macmillan, 1983.

Schongut, Emanuel. *Wake Kitten*. New York: Little Simon/Simon & Schuster, 1983.
(Other titles in the Kitten Board book series: *Look Kitten*, *Play Kitten*, *Hush Kitten*, *Catch Kitten*.)

Slobodkina, Esphyr. *Caps for Sale*. Reading, Mass.: Addison-Wesley, 1947.

Testa, Fulvio. *If You Take a Pencil*. New York: Dial, 1982.

Wells, Rosemary. *Max's Bath*. New York: Dial, 1985.
(Other titles in this series: *Max's Bedtime*, *Max's Breakfast*, *Max's New Suit*, *Max's Toys*, *Max's Ride*, *Max's First Word*.)

Wildsmith, Brian. *Brian Wildsmith's Mother Goose*. New York: Watts, 1964.

Withall, Sabrina. *The Baby's Book of Babies*. New York: Harper & Row, 1983.

You Do It Too. London: Brimax, 1979.
(Other titles in the Tiny Tots series: *All by Myself*, *Sharing*, *All Together*, *Counting Rhymes*, *Saying Rhymes*, *Singing Rhymes*.)

Zemach, Harve. *Mommy Buy Me a China Doll*. New York: Farrar, Straus & Giroux, 1975.

Ziefert, Harriet. *Baby Ben's Go Go Book*. New York: Random House, 1984.
(Other titles available in this series.)

Zion, Gene. *Harry the Dirty Dog*. New York: Harper & Row, 1956.

Zokeisha. *Mouse House*. New York: Little Simon/Simon & Schuster, 1983.
(Other titles available in the Chubby Shape book series.)

Zolotow, Charlotte. *Some Things Go Together.* New York:
  Harper & Row, 1983.

BIBLIOGRAPHY

453. Aukerman, Robert C. *Approaches to Beginning Reading,*
  2nd ed. New York: Wiley, 1984.

  As the title indicates, this volume is a compendium
  of the many approaches to beginning reading. Organized
  in encyclopedic form, the author gives both the origins
  of each approach and the background of the originators
  of the various materials and methods. In addition,
  there are complete descriptions of the methods and
  materials together with illustrations of the essential
  features of each approach.

454. Berg, Leila. *Reading and Loving.* Boston: Routledge &
  Kegan Paul, 1976.

  It is said that learning to read is the most significant intellectual achievement in a child's developmental
  progress. Along with many leaders in the field of children and reading, Berg believes that the emphasis must
  be on the instillment of love for books, rather than on
  the teaching of reading as an academic or technical
  skill. She traces the varied ways babies learn communication skills and the crucial role books have in a
  process that leads to a lifelong connection of reading
  and pleasure.

455. Bettelheim, Bruno, and Karen Zelan. *On Learning to
  Read: The Child's Fascination with Meaning.* New York:
  Knopf, 1982.

  When reading is presented to children as a mere skill
  in decoding, along with repetitive drills, they often,
  according to the authors, are actually held back from
  learning. Bettelheim, the world-renowned child psychologist, writing in collaboration with his long-time asso-
  ciate at the Orthogenic School, points out that "children
  who acquire a great interest in reading in their homes
  have an easy time reading in school." This is an impor-

tant book that explores the importance of reading and
how children are enchanted by words if we let them be.

456. Bissex, Glenda. *GNYS AT WRK.: A Child Learns to Write
and Read*. Cambridge: Harvard University Press, 1980.

This fascinating case study of the author's child
from infancy through primary grades shows how a child's
writing is closely intermeshed with reading development.
With today's emphasis on early reading, Bissex's book
provides important insights.

457. Butler, Dorothy. *Babies Need Books*. New York: Atheneum,
1980.

Butler has written a warm and sensitive guide to the
use of books with infants and toddlers. The author
believes strongly that books play a crucial role in a
child's development right from the start. She discusses
the choice of picture books, gives an annotated list of
recommended titles, and at the end of each chapter suggests how to share them with babies in the most effective
way.

458. Durkin, Dolores. *Children Who Read Early: Two Longi-
tudinal Studies*. New York: Teachers College Press,
1966.

Against a background of past findings, the research
data reported in this authoritative study answers such
questions as how and why children learn to read. The
major goal was to examine reading achievements before
first grade and the personal and environmental qualities
characteristic of these early readers. Twenty years
later, this work is still relevant.

459. Dzama, Mary Ann, and Robert Gilstrap. *Getting Your
Child to Read: A Parent's Guide*. New York: Wiley,
1983.

This book is designed to familiarize parents with the
different viewpoints educators and researchers hold
about what reading is and how it should be taught.
Chapters deal with the parent's role in the reading
process, activities for infants, toddlers, and children
of nursery school age, and questions often asked by
parents about the topic of early reading and young
children. Additional information is provided about
book selection for children of various ages, recommended
organizations and magazines for parents, and a wide range

of age-appropriate activities that involve children with books and instill a love for reading.

460. Gould, Toni S. *Home Guide to Early Reading: With Reading Readiness Games and Exercises for Your Preschool Child*. New York: Walker, 1976.

Basic to this helpful book is the concept that children learn to read when the experience is an enjoyable one, based on understanding rather than memorization. It is not a book for parents who are determined to produce a so-called "superbaby," but for parents who want to recognize and encourage their child to the fullest of his/her potential without putting on pressure to perform and impress others.

461. Jeffree, Dorothy, and Margaret Skeffington. *Reading Is for Everyone: A Guide for Parents and Teachers of Exceptional Children*. Englewood Cliffs, N.J.: Prentice-Hall, 1984.

Although the subtitle states the discussion is for children with special needs, the ideas and methods described are valuable for general application. Much is said today about "superbabies," who are taught to read with flashcards from the time they are brought home from the hospital. In this book the emphasis is on *learning*, learning through the language experience approach that allows language and language/reading skills to develop naturally--firmly setting the foundation for a lifelong love of reading.

462. Kaye, Peggy. *Games for Reading: Playful Ways to Help Your Child Read*. New York: Pantheon, 1984.

In this fun book with very serious intent, the author offers over 75 games designed to help children learn how to read while having fun. Easy to follow and simple to play, these games are ideal for parents and teachers to enjoy along with the children. There is a "bingo" game to help learn vocabulary, games that train the eye and ear to see patterns of letters and sound out words. There is also a list of easy-to-read books and books for reading aloud, as well as guidelines for teachers on how to play these games in the classroom.

463. Kimmel, Margaret Mary, and Elizabeth Segel. *For Reading Out Loud! A Guide to Sharing Books with Children*. New York: Delacorte, 1983.

The message is loud and clear, "There is no substitute for reading aloud to children." Although the focus is on children of elementary and middle school age (the authors assume that parents of toddlers do not need encouragement to read aloud while parents of older children do), the insights given are helpful to parents and teachers of younger children as well.

464. McGovern, Edythe. *They're Never Too Young for Books.* Los Angeles: Mar Vista Publishing, 1980.

In addition to presenting a practical guide to the selection of books for preschoolers, the author makes suggestions for reading aloud and for using puppets and creative dramatics along with the books. The selected titles are arranged by subject and approximate age levels.

465. Norton, Donna E. *Through the Eyes of a Child: An Introduction to Children's Literature.* Columbus, Oh.: Merrill, 1983.

Although of interest to any adult concerned with the evaluation and selection of children's literature, the focus of the text is toward students in children's literature classes.

466. Taylor, Denny. *Family Literacy: Young Children Learning to Read and Write.* Exeter, N.H.: Heinemann Educational Books, 1983.

Focusing on family interaction, this book is an important contribution to the literature in the field of literacy development in young children. It is designed for educators and parents and all those who want to learn more about the interconnection of the family, the child, and literacy.

467. Trelease, Jim. *The Read-Aloud Handbook*, rev. ed. New York: Penguin, 1985.

Directed to parents, this volume emphasizes the value of reading to children from infancy to adolescence. The author is highly critical of television and advises parents to take an active role in promoting books as a major source of entertainment as well as learning. A bibliography of recommended read-aloud books is included.

468. Tucker, Nicholas. *The Child and the Book: A Psychological and Literary Exploration.* New York: Cambridge University Press, 1982.

Exploring the relationship between children and literature, the author has written a well-balanced study that discusses literature more from the psychological impact than solely looking at the literary merit. From first books, ages 0-3, to ages 11-14, the possible responses of children to books are described and should be of interest to parents and professionals concerned with the importance of reading.

RESOURCES FOR INFANCY

Hannah Nuba-Scheffler

ACTION BULLETIN
125 West 109th St.
New York, NY 10025

THE ADVOCATE
Advocates for Children of New York, Inc.
24-16 Bridge Plaza South
Long Island City, NY 11101

AMERICAN BABY
575 Lexington Ave.
New York, NY 10022

AMERICAN EDUCATION RESEARCH JOURNAL
1230 17th St., N.W.
Washington, DC 20036

AMERICAN ORTHOPSYCHIATRIC ASSOCIATION NEWSLETTER
1775 Broadway
New York, NY 10019

AMERICAN PSYCHOLOGIST
1200 17th St., N.W.
Washington, DC 20036

ANNALS OF DYSLEXIA
Orton Dyslexia Society
724 York Road
Baltimore, MD 21204

ASSOCIATION FOR CHILDREN OF NEW JERSEY NEWSLETTER
17 Academy St.
Suite 709
Newark, NJ 07102

ASSOCIATION FOR THE SEVERELY HANDICAPPED NEWSLETTER
7010 Roosevelt Way, N.E.
Seattle, WA 98115

BABY TALK
Blessing Corporation
185 Madison Ave.
New York, NY 10016

BALLOON
The Brooklyn Children's Museum
145 Brooklyn Avenue
Brooklyn, NY 11213

BIRTH
Medical Consumer Communications, Inc.
110 El Camino Real
Berkeley, CA 94705

BIRTH TO THREE
1432 Orchard St., #4
Eugene, OR 97403

BLACK CHILD JOURNAL
1426 East 49th St.
Chicago, IL 60615

BOWS AND ARROWS NEWSLETTER
7052 West Lane
Eden, NY 14057

BUILDING BLOCKS
314 Liberty St.
Dundee, IL 60118

CARING
National Committee for Prevention of Child Abuse
332 South Michigan Ave.
Suite 1250
Chicago, IL 60604

CENTER
National Center for Health Education
30 East 29th St.
New York, NY 10016

CENTER FOR PARENT EDUCATION NEWSLETTER
55 Chapel St.
Newton, MA 02160

CHILD AND ADOLESCENT SOCIAL WORK JOURNAL
Human Sciences Press
72 Fifth Ave.
New York, NY 10011

CHILD CARE
Association for Supportive Child Care
22185 Priest
Suite 119
Tempe, AZ 85282

CHILDCARE INFORMATION EXCHANGE
C-44
Redmond, WA 98052

CHILDCARE QUARTERLY
Human Sciences Press
72 Fifth Ave.
New York, NY 10011

CHILD CARRIER
Human Services Department
Child Care Resource Center
254 College St.
New Haven, CT 06510

CHILDHOOD CITY NEWSLETTER
Center for Human Environments
Graduate Center of the City University of New York
33 West 42nd St.
New York, NY 10036

CHILDHOOD EDUCATION
Association for Childhood Education International
11141 Georgia Ave.
Suite 200
Wheaton, MD 20902

CHILD PSYCHIATRY AND HUMAN DEVELOPMENT
Human Sciences Press
72 Fifth Ave.
New York, NY 10011

CHILDREN'S DEFENSE FUND
1520 New Hampshire Ave., N.W.
Washington, DC 20036

CHILDREN'S HEALTH CARE JOURNAL
Association for the Care of Children's Health
Wavely Press, Inc.
3615 Wisconsin Ave., N.W.
Washington, DC 20016

CHILDREN'S HEALTH LINE
8990 Garfield
Suite 3
Riverside, CA 92503

CHILDREN TODAY
Office of Human Development Services
Department of Health and Human Services
U.S. Government Printing Office
Washington, DC 20402

CHURCHILL FORUM
22 East 95th St.
New York, NY 10028

CITIZEN'S REPORT
Citizen's Committee for New York City, Inc.
3 West 29th St.
New York, NY 10001

CITY SCENE
P.O. Box 67683
Century City, CA 90067

CLINICAL BIOFEEDBACK AND HEALTH
Human Sciences Press
72 Fifth Ave.
New York, NY 10011

CLOSER LOOK
A Project of the Parent's Campaign for Handicapped Children
    and Youth
P.O. Box 1492
Washington, DC 20013

CONCERNED EDUCATORS ALLIED FOR A SAFE ENVIRONMENT (CEASE)
Survival Education Fund
737 Massachusetts Ave.
Cambridge, MA 02139

CORE/PAL JOURNAL
Uni-Ed Associates
P.O. Box 2343
Elberon, NJ 07740

CREATIVE CHILD AND ADULT QUARTERLY
National Association for Creative Children and Adults
8080 Spring Valley Drive
Cincinnati, OH 45236

DAY CARE AND EARLY EDUCATION
Human Sciences Press
72 Fifth Ave.
New York, NY 10011

DOUBLE TALK
P.O. Box 412
Amelia, OH 45102

EARLY CHILDHOOD DEVELOPMENT AND CARE JOURNAL
50 West 23rd St.
New York, NY 10010

EARLY YEARS
Allen Raymond, Inc.
P.O. Box 1266
Darien, CT 06820

ECEC NEWSLETTER
Early Childhood Education Council of New York City
66 Leroy St.
New York, NY 10014

EDC NEWS
Educational Development Center, Inc.
55 Chapel St.
Newton, MA 02160

EDU-LETTER
The New York State Association for Retarded Children
175 Fifth Ave.
New York, NY 10010

EFFECTIVE PARENTING
American Guidance Service
AGS Publishers Building
Circle Pines, MN 55014-1976

EQUAL PLAY
Sex Equity in Education Program of Woman's Action Alliance,
    Inc.
370 Lexington Ave.
New York, NY 10017

ERIC/EECE NEWSLETTER
College of Education
University of Illinois
805 West Pennsylvania Ave.
Urbana, IL 61801

EXCEPTIONAL CHILDREN
1920 Association Drive
Reston, VA 22091-1589

EXCEPTIONAL EDUCATION QUARTERLY
PRO-ED
5341 Industrial Oaks Blvd.
Austin, TX 78735

EXCEPTIONAL PARENT
605 Commonwealth Ave.
Boston, MA 02215

EXCHANGES
New Jersey Network on Adolescent Pregnancy
School of Social Work Center for Community Education
78 Easton Ave.
New Brunswick, NJ 08903

FAMILY AND CHILD MENTAL HEALTH JOURNAL
Human Sciences Press
72 Fifth Ave.
New York, NY 10011

FAMILY LIFE DEVELOPMENTS
Family Life Development Center
Human Development and Family Studies
Cornell University
Ithaca, NY 14853

FAMILY RESOURCE COALITION
230 North Michigan Ave.
Suite 1625
Chicago, IL 60601

FEDERAL REGISTER
Administration for Children, Youth and Families
400 6th St., S.W.
Washington, DC 20201

FEEDBACK
The Office of School Food and Nutrition Services
44-36 Vernon Blvd.
Long Island City, NY 11101

FIRST TEACHER
P.O. Box 1308T
Fort Lee, NJ 07024

FORUM NEWSLETTER
National Clearinghouse for Bilingual Education
1555 Wilson Blvd., Suite 605
Rosslyn, VA 22209

GIFTED CHILDREN MONTHLY NEWSLETTER
Gifted and Talented Publications
213 Hollydell Drive
Sewall, NJ 08080

GROWING CHILD
Dunn and Hargitt, Inc.
22 North Second St.
Lafayette, IN 47902

GROWING CHILD STORE
Dunn and Hargitt, Inc.
22 North Second St.
Lafayette, IN 47902

HIGH/SCOPE BULLETIN
High/Scope Educational Foundation
600 North River St.
Ypsilanti, MI 48197

IN CITE
Newsletter of the Library Association of Australia
376 Jones St.
Ultimo, North Australia 2007

INFANT MENTAL HEALTH JOURNAL
Human Sciences Press
72 Fifth Ave.
New York, NY 10011

INSTITUTE FOR PSYCHOANALYSIS NEWSLETTER
International Quarterly--the Journal for and by Overseas
Educators
P.O. Box 5910
Princeton, NJ 08540

INSTRUCTOR
The Instructor Publishing, Inc.
545 Fifth Ave.
New York, NY 10017

INTERCHANGE
Ontario Institute for Studies in Education
252 Bloor St. West
Toronto, Ontario M5S 1V6, Canada

INTERRACIAL BOOKS FOR CHILDREN BULLETIN
1841 Broadway
New York, NY 10023

JOURNAL OF DEVELOPMENTAL EDUCATION
Appalachian State University
College of Education
Boone, NC 28608

JOURNAL OF LEARNING DISABILITIES
Professional Press, Inc.
633 Third Ave.
New York, NY 10003

JOURNAL OF THE ASSOCIATION FOR THE SEVERELY HANDICAPPED
7010 Roosevelt Way, N.E.
Seattle, WA 98115

KEYS TO EARLY CHILDHOOD EDUCATION
1300 North 17th St.
Arlington, VA 22209

LA LECTURA EN EL MUNDO
Asociación Internacional de Lectura Representación Latino-
americana
C.Cl.24 - Sucursal 13 (1413)
Buenos Aires, Argentina

LEARNING
1111 Bethlehem Pike
Springhouse, PA 19477

LECTURA Y VIDA
Asociación Internacional de Lectura
P.O. Box 8139
800 Barksdale Road
Newark, DE 19714

LETTER FROM DR. LEE SALK
941 Park Ave.
New York, NY 10028

LIBRARY NOTEBOOK
Library for the Blind and Physically Handicapped
The New York Public Library
166 Avenue of the Americas
New York, NY 10013

MEDIA AND METHODS
American Society of Educators
1511 Walnut St.
Philadelphia, PA 19102

MENTAL HEALTH MATERIALS UPDATE
National Mental Health Association
1800 North Kent St.
Arlington, VA 22209

MOTHERING
Mothering Publications, Inc.
P.O. Box 2208
Albuquerque, NM 87103

NATIONAL INFORMATION CENTER FOR HANDICAPPED CHILDREN AND
    YOUTH
P.O. Box 1492
Washington, DC 20013

NEWSCENE
Parent Information Resource Council, Inc.
1301 East 38th St.
Indianapolis, IN 46205

NEWSLETTER OF PARENTING
Highlights for Children
2300 West Fifth Ave.
P.O. Box 269
Columbus, OH 43216

NINETY-SECOND STREET YM-YWHA
1395 Lexington Ave.
New York, NY 10028

NURTURING NEWS
187 Caselli Ave.
San Francisco, CA 94114

OAKS AND ACORNS
Parent Education Resource Center
Metropolitan State College
1006 11th St., Box 94
Denver, CO 80204

OPTIONS
P.O. Box 311
Wayne, NJ 07470

ORTON SOCIETY NEWSLETTER
Orton Dyslexia Society
80 Fifth Ave., Rm. 903
New York, NY 10011

OUR CHILDREN'S VOICE
New York State Association for Retarded Children, Inc.
393 Delaware Ave.
Delmar, NY 12054

OUTLOOK
Mountain View Publishing
2929 6th St.
Boulder, CO 80302

PARADIDDLES
P.O. Box 1348
Columbus, IN 47202

PARENT EDUCATOR
New York Foundling Hospital
1175 Third Ave.
New York, NY 10021

PARENT GUIDE
Network Corporation
P.O. Box 1084 Lenox Hill Station
New York, NY 10021

PARENTS
80 New Bridge Road
Bergenfield, NJ 07621

PARENTS AND FRIENDS FOR CHILDREN'S SURVIVAL NEWSLETTER
P.O. Box 986 Old Chelsea Station
New York, NY 10113

PARENT'S CHOICE
P.O. Box 185
Waban, MA 02168

PARENT TALK
C/O Sunshine Press
6402 East Chaparral Road
P.O. Box 572
Scottsdale, AZ 85252

PASTORAL PSYCHOLOGY
Human Sciences Press
72 Fifth Ave.
New York, NY 10011

PEOPLE TO PEOPLE
Tucson Public Library
Special Needs Service
P.O. Box 27470
Tucson, AZ 85726-7470

PERMANENCY REPORT
Child Welfare League of America
Permanent Families for Children
67 Irving Place
New York, NY 10003

PERSPECTIVES ON DYSLEXIA
Orton Dyslexia Society
724 York Road
Baltimore, MD 21204

PRACTICAL PARENTING NEWSLETTER
18318 Minnetonka Blvd.
Deephaven, MN 55391

PSYCHOLOGY TODAY
Customer Service
P.O. Box 2563
Boulder, CO 80322

R.A.S.E. REMEDIAL AND SPECIAL EDUCATION
PRO-ED
5341 Industrial Oaks Blvd.
Austin, TX 78735

REACHING CHILDREN QUARTERLY
Reaching Children Bulletin
New York Institute for Child Development, Inc.
205 Lexington Ave.
New York, NY 10016

READING: EXPLORATION AND DISCOVERY
Education Department, Box 340
University of New Orleans
New Orleans, LA 70148

READING PSYCHOLOGY
Hemisphere Publishing Corporation
1010 Vermont Ave., N.W.
Washington, DC 20005

READING TODAY--IRA
International Reading Association
800 Barksdale Road
P.O. Box 8139
Newark, DE 19711

REPORT ON PRESCHOOL PROGRAMS
Capital Publications, Inc.
1300 North 17th St.
Arlington, VA 22209

SCHOOL LIBRARY JOURNAL
R.R. Bowker Company
P.O. Box 1426
Riverton, NJ 08077

SESAME STREET PARENT'S NEWSLETTER
Nina Blink Publishers
P.O. Box 2889
Boulder, CO 80322

SEX EQUITY NEWS
Sex Desegregation Assistance Center
P.O. Box 47
Teachers College
Columbia University
New York, NY 10027

SINGLE PARENT
Parents Without Partners, Inc.
7910 Woodmont Ave.
Bethesda, MD 20814

STUDIES IN LANGUAGE
International Journal--Foundations of Language
Amsteldijk 44
P.O. Box 52519
Amsterdam, The Netherlands 1007

TOPICS IN EARLY CHILDHOOD SPECIAL EDUCATION
PRO-ED
5341 Industrial Oaks Blvd.
Austin, TX 78735

TOP OF THE NEWS
American Library Association
50 East Huron St.
Chicago, IL 60611

TOTLINE
Warren Publishing House
P.O. Box 2255
Everett, WA 98203

TRUMPET
Children's Librarians Association of Suffolk County, Inc.
The Smithtown Library, Commack Branch
Indian Head Road
Commack, NY 11725

UNSCHOOLERS NETWORK
12 Smith St.
Farmingdale, NJ 07727

WORKING WOTHER
McCall Publishing Company
3807 Wilshire Blvd.
Los Angeles, CA 90010

YOUNG CHILDREN
National Association for the Education of Young Children
1834 Connecticut Ave., N.W.
Washington, DC 20009

YOUR CHILD AND YOU
1235 Tennessee St.
Lawrence, KA 66044

YOUTH POLICY
917 G Place, N.W.
Washington, DC 20001

ZERO TO THREE
National Center for Clinical Infant Programs
733 15th St., N.W.
Suite 912
Washington, DC 20005

AUTHOR INDEX

*The roman citations are to the numbered annotations;
those in italics are page references.*

TITLE INDEX

The citations are to the numbered annotations.